FIREWORK HUMANS

FIREWORK HUMANS

Spark A Growth Mindset.
Ignite 9 Entrepreneurial Instincts.
Fuel Courage, Curiosity, Confidence, & Conviction.

JESSICA MEAD

NEW YORK

LONDON • NASHVILLE • MELBOURNE • VANCOUVER

FIREWORK HUMANS

Spark a Growth Mindset. Ignite 9 Entrepreneurial Instints,
Fuel Curiosity, Confidence, Courage, & Conviction

Published in New York, New York, by Morgan James Publishing. Morgan James is a trademark of Morgan James, LLC. www.MorganJamesPublishing.com

Proudly distributed by Ingram Publisher Services.

Morgan James BOGO™

A **FREE** ebook edition is available for you or a friend with the purchase of this print book.

CLEARLY SIGN YOUR NAME ABOVE

Instructions to claim your free ebook edition:
1. Visit MorganJamesBOGO.com
2. Sign your name CLEARLY in the space above
3. Complete the form and submit a photo of this entire page
4. You or your friend can download the ebook to your preferred device

ISBN 9781631955518 paperback
ISBN 9781631955525 ebook
Library of Congress Control Number:
2021935194

Cover and Interior Design by:
TGC Worldwide

Morgan James PUBLISHING **Builds** with... **Habitat for Humanity®** Peninsula and Greater Williamsburg

Morgan James is a proud partner of Habitat for Humanity Peninsula and Greater Williamsburg. Partners in building since 2006.

Get involved today! Visit MorganJamesPublishing.com/giving-back

DEDICATION

To Matt, Bella, and Jaxson...

You three are the reason I make myself go beyond, why I challenge my thoughts and stretch my heart, why this book has meaning, and why my life has great purpose.

You three have taught me what a gift it is, that my energy in this universe is to be a one-of-a-kind human being and to not waste it on a life of self-doubt, regret, or madness.

You are my chaos, joy, inspiration, hope, tears, laughter, and courage.

You grant me permission to be me and encourage my messy lines and imperfections.

You are the definition of love...my love.

And to all the Firework Humans out there...

May you know them,

May you grow them,

May you be them!!!!

TABLE OF CONTENTS

INTRODUCTION

WHO WOULD I BE TODAY?

DANG!! *I AM* a pretty cool human! Some would call me a firecracker. Or say that I create fireworks out of nowhere. How's that for confidence? I'm not arrogant; instead, I'm reflecting on the life that I've been able to create for myself and my family. My choice to live life by intentional design has led me to make unbelievable things come true. And none of it happened overnight. I've grown into the ME I am today and plan to keep evolving.

The question that started this book is simple. What was it in my life that allowed me to become the groovy person I am (and strive to keep evolving to be?)

It is not just about me; it's what I want for my kids and my employees. It's what I wish for every human whose orbit enters my own and the ones I will never know. I want them to make the most of their trips around the sun. I want them to continue evolving into humans who control their orbit as well.

I see sparks in people all the time—little sparks—and I love to see them ignite and explode with possibility. It's one reason I listen to my kids' dreams so intensely—both the nighttime kind and the big-goal-hopes-manifestation-board kind!

My nine-year-old son, Jaxson, inspires me. Nearly every morning, he curls up next to me or calls me to snuggle so he can tell me about his nightly adventures. "Mom, you'll never believe what I dreamed last night!"

I just sit back and listen. Sometimes his dreams are so vivid that he swears they really happened—and maybe they will.

Sometimes his dreams are quick and to the point, and other times, they ramble along like a winding road with no end in sight. I listen as long as the dream-telling requires because his imagination is one of the coolest things I have ever witnessed. I believe he's this way because he never hears, *"That isn't real," "That doesn't make sense," "You're just silly,"* or any of the typical comments we dish out to bring "reality" into their world.

One of his recent dreams was pretty fantastic! I could tell he woke up out of this one a bit excited, and it would require a big snuggle and time to talk it through. He never just delivers the dream; he is my kiddo and needs time to process. So, we talk about the *"what-ifs"* and *"wouldn't-it-be-cool-if-we-really-coulds,"* and usually, the conversation sprawls into all sorts of unusual directions.

In this dream, we were all separated in our individual snow globes with one of our pets. Each snow globe was a place that we liked or have traveled to in the past. After living in these snow globes for three long years, we finally got out. The key part was that we all came out with superpowers! Interpret that one!

When I think about him explaining every detail to me, I know that he still sees everything as a possibility. There is no ceiling or hard Nos in his world. I hope that he travels his whole life this way.

He even records some of his dreams. As of the writing of this book, he has amassed over 200 videos.

Imagine having that much faith in your dreams when you're only nine years old! Now, imagine starting company meetings like this—by asking employees to share their most recent dreams—both from sleep and ones that they hope to come true. I know, I know—this may sound a little whoo-hoo but consider this idea for a moment. Most people go to work and spend all day talking about their boss's vision and dreams for the company. They are directed to think about sales growth, tasks, revenue, customer satisfaction, and other business operations. Often, employees become less productive, innovative, and committed because, as they try to "see" the leadership team's vision, they begin to lose their own. The leadership team does not usually ask about what's essential to the employee, what they envision as a future personally and even for the company.

Imagine encouraging your team to not only dream openly for themselves but also the company. Imagine having a company YouTube page or pinboard in the office's common areas where employees showcased these dreams. If the work-family you have created felt more open to tell you their wild ideas, what could you as a leader be inspired to create? What type of success could you achieve?

Let's face it, though; most adults have lost the ability to dream like nine-year-olds.

BUT WHAT IF...

What if we created such an open atmosphere that employees felt comfortable enough to share their personal stories? How does that change things?

At my companies, we have weekly meetings with our teams, and one of the things we do is start the discussion by asking each person to share a personal and professional highlight for the week. The highlight could be a win or good news they want to share. The highlight could be reporting on a project they are proud of or a personal goal they achieved. Starting a meeting like this erases unproductive negative emotions that can destroy the overall productivity of the meeting. Instead, sharing the highlights connects them as a team, resets their mindset, engages their brains, and ultimately builds the team's functionality and health in a positive way.

One person on our leadership team will ask a different question every day. For example, if it's Friday, the inquiry might be, *"What are you most looking forward to over the weekend?"* If it's Monday, the question might be, *"What unexpectedly happened over the weekend that was great?"* If it's a Wednesday, the inquiry might be, *"What would be the coolest thing to happen in this company by next Wednesday?"* We also throw in random questions like, *"What sport do you enjoy the most?" or "What are you binge-watching right now?"*

In one morning meeting, my share was: "I am alive! Teaching our daughter how to drive has been both exciting and terrifying! To say that I get nervous is an understatement, but I am excited that she is learning to drive and gain more freedom." My professional highlight was that I was incredibly proud of Kyle and Josh, my President and VP of Automotive, and their drive to replace some of the clients we lost. "Their work is outstanding. They are on fire, and we are now in a whole new market!"

IS IT POSSIBLE?

I didn't grow up like my son—there was no one that championed my dreams.

Growing up, I always had a sense that I was the "weird one." The idea of being weird played around the outer edges of my mind as I made sense of my world: of being broke, hungry, and trying to fit in with the other kids who had a home and traditional family life. My environment dictated my perception of myself and my potential. My story is not unique; many kids grow up like this and even less fortunate. So, why am I successful today when others in the same situation or worse are not? The answer to that question is what this book is all about.

Humans all have the same potential for success. Each person, man, woman, child, mother, father, employee, leader, teacher...have a birth born growth mindset along with these little, tiny instincts. And when these instincts are nurtured, humans explode with potential.

Is it possible that we can evolve in two ways? Is it possible that a decision can shape our outcome?

Growing up, one part of me believed putting forth great effort seemed like a bad thing. If I failed, it meant I wasn't naturally smart or talented enough. If I were, I wouldn't need to try so hard, right?

> **Humans all have the same potential for success.**

Another part of my thinking told me that I was smart and talented, but I didn't feel like that was something I could rely on, necessarily.

Until I was in high school, we never had a steady home. We lived on other people's couches, weeks at a time with relatives, sometimes in cheap hotels, storage units, an apartment or house for a while (until hard times hit), and occasionally in our car. I never felt safe believing that any type of living situation was for very long. But there was something that did make me feel safe, and that was going to the beach.

My mom would take me down to the beach to play. It didn't matter where we had slept the night before or how many jobs she had; we'd go to the beach any chance we could. She'd lie down on the sand and take an hour's long nap. The beach became my babysitter. I ran around, splashed in the water, talked to people, and built sandcastles. I was free to explore without expectations. At the beach, I felt that I could be anything and anyone—a far cry from the reality of my home life. I could count on the freedom I had at the beach to dream and create my future life while my mother slept, and that was enough for me to grow up with the other uncertainty around me.

Here's the thing. The more effort I put into envisioning an unlimited future on that beach, the easier it became. My financial limitations seemed as temporary as the couch I would or would not sleep on that night. There was no one on that beach to tell me my dreams were or were not achievable. My mom was asleep.

POSSIBLE VS. REALITY

There's a moment in the movie, The Matrix, when Keanu Reeves finds out the truth about life and existence—it can't be ignored or erased from your mind. The entire composition of his world changed, and there was no going back. In the chapters

> The more effort I put into envisioning an unlimited future on that beach, the easier it became.

that follow, I will introduce you to 9 Entrepreneurial Instincts that I believe every human possesses and guide you through the process of developing these instincts into behavioral traits. These nine instincts can be nurtured through applied education and enabling people to grow more courageous, curious, confident, and consistent—to become Firework Humans.

Yes, I've accomplished a tremendous amount in less than 40 trips around the sun. From a fantastic family to multiple thriving businesses, to global travel, and hundreds of unique experiences. I'm living a super cool life, full of fireworks, and steadily controlling my orbit. But one question still remains.

Could I have accomplished MORE in the same 40 trips around the sun if I had someone consistently championing my dreams from the very beginning? On that beach?

Take a moment. Think about it. What If somebody nurtured your curiosity early on, your unique thinking was encouraged sooner, your hesitance coached into fearlessness faster, your boundaries expanded or blown away, your failures seen through different lenses—who would you be today? Hindsight is 20-20.

Throughout our journey together, I'm going to challenge you to think about several ideas and how they apply to your family, business, and maybe a life partner too.

I believe the average person has about 80 trips around the sun, and as long as I'm still orbiting, I'm going to give this world EVERYTHING I've got. For me, this journey is about fueling courage, curiosity, confidence, and conviction with a healthy dose of love thrown in. In doing so, I am sparking a growth mindset in the people around me, igniting their unlimited potential to create—what I call—a Firework Human.

PART 1

BEING A FIREWORK HUMAN

As you read this book, I encourage you to understand this: One of the greatest gifts we are given in life is the ability to transform. If we allow ourselves, we can—at any point—decide to make a change. Transformation can happen in a dramatic, sudden way or organically over time. To fight it or stay stuck or complacent is a tragedy for yourself. In the transformation or evolution of ourselves, we discover our magic, our hidden gems, and curiosity starts to bloom, and we become free to be.

In these first few chapters, I will share what I feel are foundational principles to igniting the sparks to becoming a Firework Human. Embrace new ideas, be encouraged by the familiar, and know that it's never too late for you to spark—or *be* the spark in someone else's journey!

CHAPTER 1

WE'RE ALL FUNDAMENTALLY ENTREPRENEURIAL

"The thing about growing up with Fred and George," said Ginny thoughtfully, "is that you sort of start thinking anything's possible if you've got enough nerve."

– J.K. Rowling, Harry Potter, and the Half-Blood Prince

FIREWORK HUMANS

According to MerriamWebster.com, the definition of an entrepreneur is someone who "organizes, manages, and assumes the risks of a business or enterprise," and that's certainly not incorrect. But I believe being entrepreneurial at heart is so much more and encompasses so many other qualities. We're innovative, confident, resilient, driven, and motivated. We're life-long learners, and we're pretty obsessed and passionate about what we do.

Entrepreneurs are a unique breed, indeed! We see a need and fill it. Or, with current consumerism as it is, "see a want, fill a want!" We get creative, think out of the box, and create solutions that not only relieve the pain points of a market but also provide income for ourselves and the team of people who want to be a part of what we're doing. It's a pretty cool thing.

I believe being entrepreneurial is equal to parenting. To go one step further, I believe entrepreneurialism is a fundamental human instinct, not just a type of person. Entrepreneurialism, to me, is about being able to craft your own life

3

on your own terms using the instincts that make us creative, innovative, risk-takers—the list goes on and on. These instincts, when recognized and fostered, not only produce amazing business owners but impactful world changers in various professions and life situations.

I've also observed that people tend to view humans in two distinct ways—those who "are" and those who "are not" entrepreneurial. All things being equal, I believe that most people have the potential to think and act entrepreneurially whether they ever start their own business. Being entrepreneurial is not about business.

I believe there are four components that are common to entrepreneurial behavior.

1

A MINDSET DEVELOPMENT PROCESS

This process relates to how we perceive ourselves in the world around us. We focus on the patterns we see in our experiences and how they impact us mentally and emotionally. In order to create a mindset development process, we must first understand that our mindset is created, shifted, and developed by the processes of life in systematic interactions—meaning our thinking, acting, feeling, and experiences are attached to them.

2

THE NEED TO CREATE VALUE WHERE THERE WAS NONE BEFORE

Entrepreneurs are often recognized as business owners because they "see a need, fill a need" or "see a want, fill a want" with a new product or service. However, creating value in the absence of it can be attributed to people, like teachers and how they go above and beyond for their students, or people who routinely volunteer to help with various causes, artists who create a painting, theater pieces, and other works for the enjoyment of others whether they get paid to do it or not.

3

THE ABILITY TO PUT RESOURCES TOGETHER IN UNIQUE WAYS

Anyone who is a parent can attest that raising children is always an exercise in pulling resources together in new ways, not just monetary, but in co-parenting, education, social support, special needs, and supporting their unique talents. This is crucial, especially when starting a business—the need to analyze resources all the way around and getting creative with them is key to not only starting but continuing growth.

4

THE CONSISTENT SEARCH FOR OPPORTUNITY

You've met those people that no matter what the situation is they find a way to make it better, like the friend who can always negotiate the free room upgrade, or the student that figures out how to get full credit for a part-time internship, or the employee who always hits the bonuses, or even your Uber driver who doubles as a Door Dash Delivery driver to double their hourly income. Evolving your entrepreneurial instincts does not mean you have to own a business; it means you have a great ability to do things differently.

These four components are found in every type of person, from artists to engineers to politicians to business owners. So, if we're all inherently wired to be entrepreneurial, why don't people feel they can take action and design their own life around what's exciting and meaningful to them? The person who invented the wheel was entrepreneurial—this person saw a need to move things more easily and used basic instincts to solve the problem. We all start out with these little sparks of insight, these instincts that we don't quite know what to do with. Curiosity pushes us to explore them, stretching the boundaries of our expectations.

Humans who tap into their growth mindset and entrepreneurial instincts learn how to do things that others simply do not. The sooner a human believes that anything is possible if you try, try harder, and try again, the more rapidly these sparks develop into a vision for the future, and that's where things get exciting. Upbringing, social interactions, exposure to education, training, and background experiences can speed up or slow down the development of your entrepreneurial instincts. And just like peanuts (some people are allergic, and others are not), growing up poor does not dictate success or failure. Clearly, relationships and distinctive cultural, economic, political, religious, and technological factors all play a part in mindset and how strongly developed these instincts become. If we're encouraged and mentored to explore and develop our instincts, we can turn instincts into behavior traits and master our mindset. This is how parents can raise cool, firework humans, how leaders can develop their teams, and how life partners can grow together. It's how we make every trip around the sun count—in a big way.

A SHIFT IN EDUCATION MINDSET = SUCCESS

The Near Disaster

A business associate of mine had two children—one in kindergarten, one in second grade. The second-grade teacher kept saying that the child was not where he needed to be and was going to have him tested for learning disabilities. The parents disagreed with that cookie-cutter approach and pulled him out of school. They decided to homeschool him and tested him on their own. It was no surprise to them that he had no learning disability. The class was simply moving too quickly, and the approach to reading was just not what he needed.

The parents freaked out because they felt ill-equipped to educate their child. For the last two months of the year, they put the child back in private school. The child was having the same issues they had at the first school.

Over summer, they decided they were going to tighten up on the reading comprehension (the child was struggling with his reading and understanding what he read or attaching it to things he already knew). In doing this, they now believed they could educate their child. When the next school year started, he had progressed several reading levels and was teaching his younger sibling to read. After they researched homeschooling a bit better and figured out what would work best for their child, they pulled both children out of school, and that's where they began their homeschool journey. Now, one child is 19 and has two years of college under his belt; the other child is 17 and has already earned a year's worth of college credits. As leaders, business owners, and even parents, we have to make sure that we are viewing other humans and situations with a growth mindset and a focus on how to develop people's individual success traits (those sparks inside them that need igniting.)

If you know your child is intelligent, driven, and resourceful, but only when they're interested in the subject—you already know they think differently. And that's okay! As a parent, we must look at the individual child and determine what ignites their courage curiosity, confidence, and conviction. We must think about how they can incorporate those interests in other areas that they aren't as interested in. And most importantly, we must investigate what is making them think (and behave) differently, analyze their motivation, and know when to encourage their excitement and when to redirect it. The same is true about the teams we build, the partners we curate, and the vendors we collaborate with within our professional lives.

Remember, just like there are many employee assessments and employee rewards programs to choose from, there are also many educational paths you can put your child on, including traditional (public), private, charter, homeschooling, and hybrid models, as well as supplemental. A personal relationship is no different. Firework humans, growth mindset, and encouraging the 9 entrepreneurial Instincts is a concept you can put into play for your spouse, partner, family, and business associates. Looking into the information in the next few chapters will help you better connect with the humans in your life and help you understand how to guide, support, and ignite their ability to become Firework Humans.

IGNITING ENTREPRENEURIAL INSTINCTS

As the CEO of BrandLync (a full-service digital marketing agency) and several other companies, I have worked with hundreds of employees at every level of experience, socio-economic background, and educational level. I've tested everything I've learned over the last 15 years about homeschooling, learning styles, teaching styles, and motivating kids to expand their limits and become risk-takers on my employees.

Let's look at a normal day at BrandLync, a company that promotes a growth mindset. Managers and team leads will be checking in and communicating with team members, encouraging the effort and progress forward, not staying in their office or workspace without interaction. You will find people seeking guidance or collaboration on problems. Team members are refreshing their knowledge of products and procedures and learning about other areas of the company. There is a sense of responsibility and accountability in the air. The environment feels alive—it's not a stagnant workspace. Employees can visualize their potential to grow, learn, and thrive within that company. And because of this, they feel more committed to their work.

While the responsibility lies with the CEO (ME) to set up the right environment for the growth mindset employee to thrive, make no mistake that fixed mindset employees will be challenged to succeed in this culture. My best business advice is to discover how you, the business owner, can create a growth culture and spark the growth mindset in employees that didn't grow up with it. Through the dozens of companies and hundreds of employees that my husband and business partner, Matt, and I have had over the last 22 years, we have learned that approaching our businesses with this mindset is far more effective and impactful.

Over the next several chapters, I'll talk more about a growth mindset and how to develop the entrepreneurial instincts in both your children and your employees. Sometimes, the methods are the same, while other times, they will be different. (After all, your employees aren't eight-year-olds.) At my website, JessicaMead.com, you'll find all sorts of resources you can use with your children and your employees. You can unlock these resources by going to the Member Log-In and using the password: StillOrbiting.

CHAPTER 1

REVIEW & REFLECT

REVIEW:

1. Entrepreneurialism is a fundamental human instinct.
2. The four components of entrepreneurial behavior are: a) mindset, b) the ability to create value, c) the ability to put resources together in unique ways, d) and a consistent search for opportunity.
3. Entrepreneurial instincts and growth mindsets can be developed in both your children and your employees.

REFLECT:

1. What are my entrepreneurial qualities?
2. Do I recognize them in others?
3. Am I willing to make changes necessary to nurture the growth mindset and entrepreneurial instincts in both my family and team members?

CHAPTER 2

Sparking the Flame of the Growth Mindset

There's something that every human needs to believe with every cell in their bodies. When they do, they will thrive. Period. Your brain grows stronger—exponentially so—with time put in and continuous effort.

Oh, if humans could only grasp this fully. Some do, and they do thrive. Others, whether consciously or subconsciously, don't believe this to be accurate and don't fully become all they could. And so many times, I think it comes down to one's mindset. The idea that people may have one of two mindsets was proposed by Carol Dweck.[1] a psychology professor at Stanford. Her work identified that "People adopt one of two types of mindsets: "fixed" and "growth." In a fixed mindset, people believe their basic qualities, like their intelligence or talents, are simply fixed traits. They believe that talent alone creates success. Whereas people with a more persistent growth mindset believe that they can substantially change their intelligence and personality with effort."

A growth mindset fosters motivation, resilience, and persistence. A fixed mindset kills it. Some humans believe that their mental capacity to learn things is not as strong as those people who were simply "born smarter." This belief leads them to give up quicker, believing that if they can't do something, it's because they aren't smart enough, creative enough, fair enough, or whatever enough. Humans who have a growth mindset are more likely to keep working hard toward a goal, believing that all that stands between them and success is the right amount of effort. A growth mindset moves both education and business forward and positions them for more growth, profit, and success in the future. So how do all of these puzzle pieces fit together?

From a business perspective, it starts with how I conduct the first job interview, to employee reviews, the company culture, and compensation plans. My mission is to ignite their entrepreneurial instincts and help them develop more courage, curiosity, confidence, and conviction. It has made all the difference in my business's success and the satisfaction of my team's work-life—they're not my kids, but they are my work family. As the architect and leader, I understand that it is my job to invest in everyone's success and growth. This belief is in keeping with my motivation to continually evolve, seek knowledge, and lead by example. From a parenting perspective, I've taken years to understand my children's learning style and motivation and crafted outside-of-the-box education plans that allow them to thrive without worrying about a "normal education."

> A growth mindset moves both education and business forward and positions them for more growth, profit, and success in the future.

So, let me ask you this:

- What mindset did you have growing up?
- Thinking back, did your home life or classroom experiences impact your confidence, self-worth, and motivation to try harder?

Understanding how you were raised can help you more fully develop a growth mindset as an adult.

FIXED VS. GROWTH MINDSETS

The concept of a fixed vs. growth mindset sounds simple, but the application of either can subconsciously change behavior. Some humans believe that they can adapt and grow, but others are certain that they are as they are, and nothing will change that fact. These humans grow believing this, and sadly, this influences a lifetime of choices. In Dweck's book, *Mindset: The New Psychology* Success, she explains that, while a fixed mindset assumes that our character, intelligence, and creative ability are static that we can't change in any meaningful way. A growth mindset thrives on challenge and sees failure "not as evidence of unintelligence but as a heartening springboard for growth and for stretching our existing abilities."

Let's take a closer look at how both the fixed and growth mindsets operate regarding six key areas: Persistence, Challenges, Confidence, Failure, the Willingness to Seek Help, and Learning Styles. As you review these, it's essential to understand that, as humans, we are not 100% one way or the other. We all have triggers and can slide from a growth to a fixed mindset from time to time. It's what we do with this knowledge that changes our journey.

> We all have triggers and can slide from a growth to a fixed mindset from time to time. It's what we do with this knowledge that changes our journey.

PERSISTENCE

Have you seen how some people will keep trying because they must figure something out, while others will give up after one or two failed attempts? You might naturally think that the person who keeps trying has a growth mindset, and the person who gives up has a fixed mindset. And you might be wrong. Here's why. My kiddos are very different in how they approach things and navigate life. My daughter is the one who will tackle something repeatedly until she has it solved or comes to a solution she deems satisfactory, using the clues from each failed attempt to guide her through the next effort. This pattern shows she has a persistent growth mindset. My son also personifies a growth mindset but will often get defeated after the second failed attempt and move on. Here, a fixed mindset is triggered, and his Try Again entrepreneurial instinct is still underdeveloped. The same thing will happen with adults; some will wear a problem out and pull in resources until it's solved.

Others will try once or twice and just assume they won't ever solve the problem and abandon it. Once either of these options becomes the normal pattern, it creeps into other areas of their lives. One of the hardest parts about understanding mindset is being able to step out of yourself and take a bird's-eye view and honestly analyze who you are and how you function in life. Only then can you truly see your patterns and triggers and start to figure out if they align with the life you desire. Try it. The next time you leave a meeting, get in a heated conversation or one you deem positive, hit a roadblock, get frustrated with your spouse, get upset at your child's behavior, really anything in your life, grab a notepad and take 5 minutes to step out of your head and analyze what just happened. Be honest with yourself and hold yourself accountable like you do others in your orbit. Write down the parts that were creating solutions and moving in a positive direction, and write down what had you stuck in the problem, what fed the fire, and what kept you aggravated?

Now how much was you and how much was them? Look it over and figure out how you could have course-corrected not only your response/reaction but helped guide the other person. We all do a mini version of this in our head, over and over again when we have an argument—"I should have said this," or "I should have responded this way"—but often we are responding to the other person and not to ourselves. You see, once we start to understand how we lead ourselves down a destructive path or throw up roadblocks for ourselves, we can clearly see that it's easier to self-sabotage than move forward at times—so we do it. Then, it becomes part of our norm. If you start living in the solution, learn how to recognize and navigate what triggers you, and help others see that you are willing, they will follow suit.

CHALLENGES

Ever heard the phrase, "They took the easy way out," referring to people who choose easy over better? If you have a fixed mindset choosing the easy solution comes naturally to you because you don't think about more challenging options that may produce better results—because what if you fail? If you apply this to a work environment, you can quickly see how this behavior can be costly to the bottom line. Imagine John in your company ordering office supplies from the same vendor without ever checking if other suppliers have the exact supplies at a better price or if there is a more cost-efficient way to buy them.

On the one hand, John can say, "Well, we always order from this vendor, they haven't changed their prices, and I didn't have to delay by getting accounting to approve a new vendor." On the other hand, John can think, "I found the same office supplies at a different vendor for 20% less, and all I need to do to take advantage of the savings is get accounting to set up an account. Then I will have two options for office supplies and can take advantage of the best prices regardless of the vendor." When I state it like this, everyone reading thinks that John should do the latter, but when you think about your co-workers or employees, you can point out many examples when John did the easy thing. It's the same with our children. As parents, we often set them up to avoid challenges, and here's how; we do everything for them, and when we do have them try something or figure it out, we get frustrated with the amount of time it is taking them and step in and just do it for them.

I know families where the children never do a single thing for themselves. Instead of allowing them the time to get frustrated and keep trying so that they develop a solutions-driven problem-solving mindset, parents often step in and or don't even allow them that option. Those same parents who do everything find that as their children become young adults, they start using terms like lazy and lacks ambition or respect, but in reality, they created that person. Parents, leaders, spouses, all human beings need to understand that progress is power; allowing them the ability to create progress of any kind is giving them the power to take action and to create a pattern towards solutions. Allowing the humans in your orbit (business or personal) to fall back on a fixed mindset is not how you create the most dynamic network of Firework Humans possible. Additionally, not encouraging others to grow their entrepreneurial instincts leaves very little room for the vulnerability needed to learn and grow. It's important to show them that learning is all about starting at the edge of our capabilities and pushing beyond them. Humans with a growth mindset embrace challenge. It is an opportunity to learn, grow, and do more.

> Learning is all about starting at the edge of our capabilities and pushing beyond them.

CONFIDENCE

If success means you are smart, then a lack of success means they're dumb. This belief is the case for humans who grew up with a fixed mindset. If a person enters into a problematic situation with a fixed mindset, they are more likely to believe they don't have what it takes to get through it. On the other hand, humans with a growth mindset are less afraid to tackle the unknown with fewer reservations about failing. The sad thing is that left unchecked, a fixed mindset compounds over their life and can lead to a lack of ambition, learning new things, and lowered motivation.

As a leader or parent, praising humans for their effort over the outcome is one way to nurture a growth mindset. Regardless of age, when coming up short on a difficult task or situation, if a human is used to hearing, "You worked hard on this, thank you," no matter the outcome, the takeaway is that win or lose, their efforts are of value. The reverse would be a human who is used to hearing, "You did it. Great job!" only after having success. The difference is that we champion a growth mindset over a fixed mindset. It's not just about telling or showing them they are successful; it's also that they are significant.

> It's not just about telling or showing them they are successful; it's also that they are significant.

FAILURE

For humans with a growth mindset, failure isn't a bad thought because they are open to trying again and figuring out a different path. Their self-worth is not linked to absolutes like success or failure. One of the reasons I am continually fostering a growth mindset in my employees is because it encourages them to have a healthy attitude towards failure, which allows them to present new solutions to problems that serve the best interest of the company. Even when something doesn't work out the first time, their confidence stays up, and they know they'll succeed if they keep working at it. Is this not something to strive to support our employees and co-workers?

SEEKING HELP

Whether it is your child asking for help on homework or an employee raising their hand and asking for support to get the job done, both are examples of a growth mindset. In a fixed mindset situation, a child or employee will be more likely to hide their struggles, lie about their mistakes, or shy away from opportunities they don't believe they can handle. In a fixed mindset, mistakes equal "stupid" or incapable. On the other side, humans with a growth mindset don't associate asking for help as a weakness but as a way to get something done more efficiently. Where our children and employees "fail" is in being too embarrassed or scared to try and fail, fail and ask for help, and try again until they master it. As leaders or parents, we must continuously and consistently assure them this is not true.

LEARNING STYLES

If humans have a fixed mindset with underdeveloped entrepreneurial instincts, then in traditional school, learning challenges like dyslexia, ADHD, slow reader, and visual over auditory learner may suppress their love of learning. With these examples, this feeling can also impact their participation and increase anxiety and pessimism surrounding education. It is valid for both children in school and employees trying to succeed at work.

If humans have a growth mindset with well-developed entrepreneurial instincts, then traditional education may not impact them negatively. Of course, this does not necessarily mean that they are pushing to reach their potential either.

When deciding on the optimal educational path for your child, you need to look at their current mindset and how standardized testing, grading systems, and classroom learning styles help or hinder them. With your employees, you need to decide which communication, training, and accountability systems foster a growth mindset. When determining if you have the right employees in the right positions, you need to look at their learning style, any hidden skills they possess, their upbringing (if known), mindset, and how your company culture supports or works against them. Education does not stop at school. It is every human's job to foster continuous learning for everyone in their orbit.

> Where our children and employees "fail" is in being too embarrassed or scared to try and fail, fail and ask for help, and try again until they master it.

CHAPTER 2

REVIEW & REFLECT

REVIEW:

1. A growth mindset fosters motivation, resilience, and persistence.
2. In a fixed mindset, people believe their basic qualities, like their intelligence or talents, are simply fixed traits.
3. It's essential to understand that, as humans, we are not 100% one way or the other. We all have triggers and can slide from a growth to a fixed mindset from time to time. It's what we do with this knowledge that changes our journey.

REFLECT:

1. Did you grow up with a fixed mindset or a growth mindset? How has that affected you in your adult life?
2. Have you changed as an adult?
3. Can you see these traits in your children or employees?

CHAPTER 3

THE POWER OF LANGUAGE

WORDS MATTER

Your words matter when it comes to igniting courage, curiosity, confidence, and conviction in the humans in your orbit. Focusing your words on praise for being intelligent promotes a fixed mindset.[2] Focusing your comments on recognition for being resilient promotes a growth mindset. In business, we often hear words like "Great work" or "Nice report." Even though this sounds like positive encouragement, it lacks the specific words needed to make a fixed mindset employee feel empowered to tackle the bigger picture. In contrast, the recognition that focuses on effort, like, "You've worked really hard on that!" or "You've put a lot of effort into this," promotes a growth mindset.

In my companies, I say things like: *"The solution you came up with was impressive, and I appreciate you taking ownership of the problem."*

"You brought me three solutions, which tells me you really put a lot of effort into solving this independently, and I appreciate it so much. Let's go with solution X."

This takes a little more effort to do in business because we often feel silly engaging or interacting longer than a quick word or two. The key here is to make an effort every time you communicate to recognize the action and explain why you feel the way you do and how it impacts the work, client, etc. This is necessary for positive praise and correcting an employee for something done incorrectly or getting lost in their task. It can sound like:

- *"Great job on the new reports!"* **vs.** *"Wow, Kristen! You have really streamlined those reports. The way you have set them up now makes everyone more efficient and less likely to make mistakes. I really* *appreciate you taking the initiative to dive into that and working with your team to make this better."*

- *"Ryan, you keep making errors. Fix it, or you may not have a place here."* **vs.** *"Ryan, I noticed you are struggling to make sure the client's artwork is free of errors before it goes to them for final approval. Is there something we can do to help you? Are you overwhelmed or just trying to get through it too fast? Maybe I can jump in and lend a hand to triage and get you back on track?"*

It starts with you. The language we use with ourselves is also very important because self-talk can make or break you. Pay attention to how you use words and the ones you choose. What nouns and verbs do you use to define yourself? List them out and now think about each one. Do you feel good or bad about each word? Which one(s) would you want to change? When you work to change those words, this will flow into all areas of your life, and you will start to see how the words we choose for ourselves and for others have a profound effect on our lives. Ultimately understanding that the language we use with ourselves and the people we interact with is key to a growth mindset.

Self-talk can make or break you.

NEVER UNDERESTIMATE YOUR IMPACT

My family finds the people who gravitate to me amusing. Every time I find myself standing near a stranger, I make a conscious choice to speak to them, ask questions, and look beyond their words into the meanings they hold in their hearts. It's an urge, and I can't fight it because I am curious and confident in my courage to engage. I seek to know, to understand, to relate. We can be anywhere—from a grocery store to a cross-country flight—and I always seem to connect to someone who has a need. Sometimes it's just the connection and listening to their story, or they were listening to me talk and were curious and seeking more information.

There is power in conversation. I discovered early on in life that I have this unique ability to see things—qualities in people—that they do not yet see in themselves. Joy, fascination, child-like wonder, talent, creativity...whatever it may be, is usually unveiled in even short conversations. I suppose there could be many reasons why this happens. I believe it is my willingness to bring my whole, authentic self to each conversation. I listen and feel deeply. I share bits of who I am in an even exchange of openness, hoping to add value somehow.

One particular time, I was on a flight from Orlando to Houston; we left Walt Disney World and stopped to visit some friends and family in Texas on our way home. My kiddos were in the two seats in front of me. I was seated next to a man who'd just left a convention where he'd won an award for his efforts with a big company. He was headed home to New Zealand, and Houston was just a stop on his way. This man was massively successful and a superstar in his industry; I was the "mom" in her Disney clothes. Something I said ignited curiosity for him, and he started up a conversation. We spent the next 2.5 hours talking about business, family, and life. It was an excellent conversation for both of us.

I got off the plane, and he continued his travels. I had given him my Instagram handle to reach out about any of the business things we discussed. (I didn't have any business cards and don't give out my info.) When he landed at home, he sent me a message thanking me because he said our talk helped him through his long flight. He was trying to remember something specific I had told him—the three things I encourage and ask people in my orbit to carry with them each day: courage, confidence, and love. That was it.

Fast forward a few months. *"Hi, Jessica. I hope all is well. I just wanted to let you know the impact you had on a stranger on that brief flight we shared from Orlando to Houston a few months back. You captured in 3 words the ethos I take to my workplace every day and look for in my teams, and in doing so, gave me the script and paused to review my life. While I had, in my carry-on luggage, an award recognizing me as a top leader amongst 31,000 employees, it simultaneously made me realize I had not delivered my courage, confidence, and love as equal to my family. This week, I have resigned from my position after 20 years in the industry. I accepted a role that reduces my need to travel on 100 flights per year. This decision will give me back 15 hours per week, all in favor of more time with*

Words are powerful.

my wife and daughter. Words are powerful, so thanks for sharing that short flight in conversation with a stranger."

When I read this, my first thought was, "MAY-DAY!" This man took my words and changed his whole life! I broke out in a sweat and panicked for a bit. I suddenly felt responsible if his life took a wrong turn or his new venture failed. But then I realized all I did was ignite what was already inside him, what he already knew and felt, and all I did was give him the subtle push to course-correct and change his path. He has put my words on his wall in his new company, and it is one of the biggest compliments of my life.

Bam! That is a Firework Human!

You never know who needs a champion or a conversation that creates sparks inside them. My goal in life is to be that person for everyone and anyone who needs it. Words have the power to change lives. I desire to make each word count, intentionally nudge people along, find their strength, fulfill their needs, and help them achieve their brand of success. This is why I wrote this book. To support each of you, whether you're a parent, business owner, teacher, leader or wanderer, create more Firework Humans at every step of your lives.

CHAPTER 3

REVIEW & REFLECT

REVIEW:

1. Your words matter when it comes to igniting courage, curiosity, confidence, and conviction in the humans in your orbit.
2. Recognition that focuses on effort promotes a growth mindset.
3. Understanding that the language we use with ourselves and the people we interact with is key to a growth mindset.

REFLECT:

1. What does your self-talk sound like?
2. Think about how you use words and the ones you choose. Are they filled with hope and growth potential, or are they negative, providing little room for growth?
3. What can you say to your child, partner, or employees to provide encouragement and growth today?

CHAPTER 4

SUPPORTING A GROWTH MINDSET

I believe any organization that adopts a growth mindset can position itself to thrive. At BrandLync, we operate by a set of attitudes and behaviors that reflect the belief that an individual's talent can grow and evolve; nothing is set in stone. Skill can be developed. Intelligence can be fostered. Creativity and innovation can be strengthened. Leaders can emerge. People hold potential. My leadership team incorporates these principles into company meetings, compensation plans, promotion requirements, internal communication, and how we encourage each other. We always recognize the effort of our colleagues. We spread the word to others to recognize when someone is going above and beyond. This means every employee within my organization has to have the ability to develop, grow, and learn. If more companies worked to help each of their employees succeed, become better leaders, take on more leadership capabilities, and continuously evolve their skills and thinking, we as a global community would thrive.

> If more companies helped their employees succeed and continuously evolve their skills and thinking, we as a global community would thrive.

Here are five things I learned—while homeschooling and running companies at the same time—that promote a growth mindset.

HIRE THOSE WHO LOVE TO LEARN

Finding people who love to learn, who are open to trying new things and new ways and understand there's more than one way to accomplish something is key to fostering a growth mindset company. In business, I find that as someone's level of expertise increases, the more they struggle to see new solutions or ideas. There's less thinking outside of the box. They don't see through multiple lenses and learning stalls, which leads businesses to get stuck in their thinking. (The same thing happens with children in school.) This also happens as businesses scale—employees cling to tried-and-true ways because fast scaling often brings on overwhelming amounts of work. The key here is to watch for this and make sure your team is not drowning and that hiring happens along the way to ensure your growth culture is still alive and thriving.

> To promote a growth mindset that will propel your organization's forward momentum, it's essential to focus on people's capacity and not their pedigree.

Most companies hire the moment they are overwhelmed and have no choice but to add another human to the bus. We hire in anticipation of that moment so that we are not merely sticking a person in that seat but finding the right person to add value and complement the culture of the team she or he is joining. To promote a growth mindset that will propel your organization's forward momentum, it's essential to focus on people's capacity and not their pedigree. As such, it's vital to value those who show a substantial commitment to learning. These people will help instill a learning culture, quickly and successfully collaborating with others no matter what command comes their way. Individuals who show a capacity and drive to keep learning have a natural mindset, hugely valuable to business success.

ENCOURAGE NEW SKILL DEVELOPMENT

Developing new skills—even if they shift outside of someone's current work responsibilities—is always valuable. After all, understanding and learning roles other than your own promotes empathy, collaboration, and encourages new ways of approaching things. I also believe that it is key to making your employees more productive and inspired at work. The key is to make sure they can participate in activities, tasks, or projects not in their job description. This can be as simple as letting them listen in on a client call, as elaborate as sending them to advanced training or asking them to represent your company at a trade show. They will learn and grow more confident and convicted to you and your company. Again, progress is power. Employees don't need to be the CEO to run the company. They just have to be encouraged to fill in the blanks, so the CEO's vision comes true; that's the magic.

> *"Courage is not the absence of fear, but rather the judgment that something else is more important than fear."*
>
> **– Meg Cabot.**

FIREWORK HUMANS DON'T ALWAYS SPARKLE – AND THAT'S OK

As business owners, we often limit our team's ability to make independent decisions, fearing that their mistakes could cost us customers and money. Championing a growth mindset means accepting that failure is inevitable to achieve growth. As a business owner, I found that one of the hardest things to do was give my team the freedom to make mistakes. A part of it was pride in my reputation. Another aspect of it was the worry of lost revenue and costly mistakes. It took a few companies and a few different teams transitioning to get comfortable with letting individuals learn and grow through making mistakes—even when it costs the company money. Of course, it freaked me out, but I needed to homeschool my kids, so I had to take a leap of faith and allow my team to run the company if I wanted the extra time to directly work on my children's education. I had no idea that it would empower my team and foster a sense of steadfast loyalty to me and commitment to the company. The experience made me want to be a better leader and help my employees grow in the same way I was nurturing my children. So, I set out to discover more ways to support my teams in accomplishing things without my direct oversight (take risks without fear of failure) without jeopardizing my company.

Championing a growth mindset means accepting that failure is inevitable to achieve growth.

When you are trying to take a start-up to the next level or scale, accepting that, at some point, you will fail, or your employees will misstep, or things will just not go right, will make things easier. Propelling a business forward through innovation and creativity is possible if you're willing to take risks. Risk-taking and the tolerance for failure need to start with the head of the household or the leadership team. Whether you are parenting or inspiring your team, setting the example allows employees and children to take on leadership roles—with the mental freedom to try things, fail, and learn from their mistakes.

FUEL COMMITMENT AND INNOVATION

Employees at growth mindset companies feel more committed to their work as they think they have the potential to grow, learn, and thrive within it. They are more motivated to do their best because they know that they are valued for their personal development and hard work. If you have children, you can appreciate this thinking. Kids always feel empowered when they are asked to make the decisions and encouraged to try again. One way I encourage this is that I don't accept "I don't care, you decide" as a response. (We all know this one because it's one of the most used lines for children!) I often do it with a lighthearted approach, like, "Ok then, we will have water for dinner!" or something obnoxiously opposite of what they would like. We laugh, and they know they have to contribute to the conversation!

Research has also shown that employees at growth mindset organizations pursue more innovative projects, are more transparent, cut fewer corners, and work more collaboratively. And these authentically motivated people will drive innovation and fuel business.[3] Do you want to position your company to meet its goals and objectives and continually move forward? Then you need to adopt a growth mindset. You need to see the opportunity and potential in every moment. You'll be developing, advancing, and expanding your team—and company—along with it. A growth mindset will propel your business forward and position you, your brand, and people for growth, profit, and success.

> **You need to see the opportunity and potential in every moment.**

INTENTIONAL CONGRUENCE

Intentional congruence is how Matt and I have designed our life. It wasn't always that way, but over time, it organically shifted to this idea, this coming together of all the important things in our lives to work in harmony and create balance. There is this idea that in order to be successful, you have to sacrifice in other areas, like family. In order to have a successful family life, you must sacrifice your career. The idea with intentional congruence is to find ways to align as many things as possible in your life so they work together —to simplify and combine to get the most out of your time. You will also notice the symbiotic relationship the different parts of your life have, and you will start to shed what is not serving you, your family, and your business. This helps us flow through life as a unit and not separate pieces—with boundaries in place so we don't allow people or circumstances to blur our vision.

> The idea with intentional congruence is to find ways to align as many things as possible in your life so they work together.

CHAPTER 4

REVIEW & REFLECT

REVIEW:

1. Any organization that adopts a growth mindset can position itself to thrive.

2. If more companies worked to help each of their employees succeed, become better leaders, take on more leadership capabilities, and continuously evolve their skills and thinking, we as a global community would thrive.

3. Five things you can do to promote a growth mindset in your company include: a) hire those who love to learn; b) encourage skill development; c) accept that failure is a part of growth; d) fuel innovation; e) simplify and combine to make the most of your time.

REFLECT:

1. Think of one simple change you can make today that will help promote a growth mindset in your workplace or with your children? How can you implement it?

2. How can you foster an environment where it's ok to make mistakes?

3. What is one thing you can simplify to make the most of your time—at home and at work?

CHAPTER 5

DOES CHILDHOOD MATTER?

UPBRINGING AND ITS IMPACT ON FUTURE MINDSET

I felt like a chapter like this needed to be in the book because most people use their childhood and upbringing as a crutch or a pedestal. I think the takeaway from any childhood should be the lessons learned. When Matt and I decided we wanted to have a child, there were many difficult conversations about how we wanted to raise children. Having both come from challenging childhoods, we aligned on some things and were apart on others. We found ourselves economically aligned with the middle class, but there were strong feelings about the benefits of how we were raised in relation to being on the low socio-economic side.

Looking at our kids now, I will say they are a healthy blend—a blend I feel good about and see as a nice balance of both worlds. We are at a place where we could give our kids the world on a silver platter, but we don't because we understand the consequences and want them to feel how great it is to earn and give back. We want them to be global citizens who love and respect the world and all who inhabit it. We want them to have growth mindsets with empathy and compassion and a strong drive to keep moving forward in life. I want to create awareness for the readers who are parents, so they understand the benefits and the negatives of both ways and encourage all parents to design a path that works for their goals, hopes, and dreams for their children. I want all readers to look at their upbringing and encourage them to live in the lessons and not use it as an excuse, a crutch, or a pedestal.

Believe it or not, our upbringing plays a significant role in determining our mindset. Think about your childhood. What types of opportunities did you have when you were a child?

- Did you take piano or dance lessons after school, or did you play out in the yard with the neighbor kids until your parent(s) came home?
- Did you have private tutoring lessons after school, or did you have to tough it out in school until you figured it out (or the teacher moved on)?
- Did you live in an affluent area and have access to good schools, or did you just go to the school in your neighborhood area?
- Did your parents set education expectations for you, or was education left to the teachers without your parents' involvement?
- Did your parents assert themself when it came to your health, or did they just follow what the doctor told them was best?

These questions do make us think. The answers are neither right nor wrong, better nor worse. It points to two different parenting styles: whether by choice or necessity, our upbringing, and how we're raising our children now. I resonate with sociologist Annette Lareau[4], who addresses these questions' importance in her book, *Unequal Childhoods*.[5] The book discusses the different parenting approaches of concerted cultivation and the accomplishment of natural growth, examining the parenting style differences between middle class, working-class, and low-income parents—and what it does to a child's future. The book hit home because when you are trying to raise or lead Firework Humans using a growth mindset and encouraging the 9 Entrepreneurial Instincts, understanding the difference a childhood set of experiences has on a human is critical.

> **Understanding the difference a childhood set of experiences has on a human is critical.**

I'm not one of these motivational speakers who says, "Your background doesn't matter. You can be anyone you want regardless of how much money you had growing up." I recognize that I was raised in a "natural growth" family and that my life (how I thought, the choices I made, the risks I took) could have landed me in a very different place. However, If I had let my past dictate my future, I'd be starving right now. It's why understanding when to "structure versus unstructured" your child's or your employee's day is significantly important.

Mindset is everything. You can't fully develop a growth mindset without first acknowledging the socio-economic impact of your early years. Understanding this about yourself and your employees will make you a better leader. Understanding your family's opportunities and limitations will help you make the right choice in guiding your child's educational journey by knowing what to supplement and support them with learning and exposure to different activities.

CONCERTED CULTIVATION

Concerted cultivation is a middle-class approach to parenting that involves the deliberate cultivation of a child's development. In this situation, a family will put their children in the best schools and structure all their activities. The parents are prepping their children in all the ways to succeed. They are providing a success roadmap, and the children are not making decisions for themselves. Lareau found that parents were very involved in overseeing their children's success in both white and black middle-class families, including monitoring their academics and being very active in their lives. Lareau also found that middle-class children participated in several different activities, were required to spend significant time on homework, and often had many extracurricular obligations, like playing sports or practicing an instrument. Therefore, middle-class lives were often hectic. In many ways, concerted cultivation gives children an advantage because it aligns with the professional world's demands. But it can also lead to a fixed mindset and underdeveloped entrepreneurial instincts.

NATURAL GROWTH

On the other hand, natural growth does not always provide for this same opportunity. Lareau found that children from middle-class families simply have more options due to their economic resources. When Lareau visited the homes of low-income and working-class families, she observed that a lack of financial resources made enrolling their children in extracurricular activities challenging. Both white and black poor and working-class family kids played outside with neighbors more, and they were responsible for themselves. These children also did not receive as much academic attention at home, which often created school challenges. Working-class and poor parents often work long hours or hold multiple jobs simply to support the family. In some families, food shortages were more common. Economic inequality makes giving children the same opportunities as their middle-class counterparts rough. There are exceptions, but you get my point.

Many parents in natural growth situations can't afford extra activities or private schools, so they leave it up to the teachers, neighbors, and relatives to fill in the gaps. A positive aspect of a natural growth approach is that families have more cookouts and hang out, play, and eat together—because it does not require them to spend money at a restaurant. This scenario is fantastic for teaching lessons, passing down generational history, and bonding. These kinds of activities dictate how they step out into the world as human beings. A natural growth approach often forces the evolution of entrepreneurial instincts and a growth mindset because there is more freedom to explore during the day, fewer structured learning/activities, and having to keep yourself entertained can ignite creativity. There are both advantages and disadvantages to both approaches.

> A natural growth approach often forces the evolution of entrepreneurial instincts and a growth mindset.

HERE IS A SIMPLE CHART THAT BREAKS DOWN THE DIFFERENCES:

CHILD-REARING APPROACH

	CONCERTED CULTIVATION	ACCOMPLISHMENT OF NATURAL GROWTH
KEY ELEMENTS	Parent actively fosters and assesses child's talents, opinions, and skills	Parent cares for child and allows child to grow
ORGANIZATION OF DAILY LIFE	Multiple child leisure activities orchestrated by adults	"Hanging out," particularly with kin, by child
LANGUAGE USE	Reasoning/directives Child contestation of adult statements	Directives Rare questioning or challenging of adults by child General acceptance by child of directives
INTERVENTIONS IN INSTITUTIONS	Criticisms and interventions on behalf of child Training of child to take on this role	Dependence on institutions Sense of powerlessness and frustration Conflict between child-rearing practices at home and at school
CONSEQUENCES	Emerging sense of entitlement on the part of the child	Emerging sense of constraint on the part of the child

SOURCE: *Unequal Childhoods* by Annette Lareau

Imagine what harnessing your child's or your employee's mindset will do for their ability to succeed at anything life throws them. As an employer and leader, listening and picking up on the clues that my staff give me about their upbringing allows me to cultivate a plan as to how I can help them in their journey for growth and to see where they could possibly be struggling. It allows me to see where their strengths and weaknesses are. This not only benefits them but the company as a whole. Investing in any human, whether an employee, child, family member, or friend, is always worth the time and effort. Go to JessicaMead.com and download my 25 Ways to Nurture a Child's Growth Mindset and 25 Ways to Unleash Your Team's Growth Mindset.

CHAPTER 5

REVIEW & REFLECT

REVIEW:

1. You can't fully develop a growth mindset without first acknowledging the socio-economic impact of your early years. Understanding this about yourself and your employees will make you a better leader.

2. Concerted cultivation is a middle-class approach to parenting that involves the deliberate cultivation of a child's development. Parents prepare their children in all the ways to succeed, and the children are not necessarily making decisions for themselves.

3. Many parents in natural growth situations can't afford extra activities or private schools, so they leave it up to teachers, neighbors, and relatives to fill in the gaps. A natural growth approach often forces the evolution of entrepreneurial instincts and a growth mindset because there is more freedom to explore during the day, fewer structured activities, and having to keep yourself entertained can ignite creativity.

REFLECT:

1. Think back to your childhood. Which way do you think you were raised?

2. How do you think that has benefited you today?

3. How do you think that has affected the way you are raising your children—or are managing your employees?

CHAPTER 6

THE 9 ENTREPRENEURIAL
INSTINCTS

My entrepreneurial instincts made me fearless—but let's face it, I didn't have much to lose anyway. I had the spirit and the abilities but no real formal training and encouragement on how to use them. I developed courage out of hope, confidence out of necessity, curiosity out of desperation, and conviction from a lack of choices. So, you can say that my childhood forced this evolution of my entrepreneurial journey and gave me the four big Cs—Courage, Curiosity, Confidence, and Conviction.

So, let's explore the 9 entrepreneurial Instincts that I believe we are all born with and how to nurture them into consistent behavioral traits. Each of these instincts will be highlighted in its own chapter later in the book, but here's an introduction to each one.

THE KNOWLEDGE SEEKING INSTINCT

This instinct is about continually learning. Reading, thinking, listening, observing, absorbing, and applying are all trademarks of a great leader. A love of learning can help every natural instinct be discovered and developed. How your child or your employees emotionally feel about learning new things determines their level of success. History shows a pattern of this specific instinct being hyper-developed in individual humans that caused significant advancements like the light bulb, air travel, and space travel. A great way to encourage this instinct and all the others is leadership through action; show them that you are willing and capable to take action and do all these things.

THE AUDACIOUS DREAMER INSTINCT

The Audacious Dreamer instinct is about doing what you love and are passionate about in life. Children instinctually start off as audacious dreamers, seeing no limits and exuding creativity. Tapping into how to remain an audacious dreamer despite educational systems and governing policies is important and necessary to grow this vital instinct that forms the backbone of successful entrepreneurship. Encouraging this instinct in your employees will ignite big passion and vision-building in them. Take the time to share with your employees, family, and friends your audacious dreams. Make a point to share the ones you have had at all stages in your life and how you achieved them. Share your story of failure and then success, then let them see and experience it through your words. I find that when I do this, it creates a unity between myself and the person I am talking to—a sort of accountability forms to check on each other to make sure we are continuously working towards our dreams. It also shows them that fear didn't shackle you, and you found a way to keep moving forward.

THE TRY-AGAIN INSTINCT

This instinct is about being resilient. We are born resilient, and resiliency is a buildable skill that can grow with time. Humans want to attain goals. And yet, so many give up when faced with failure. Left to our own devices, we contract and retreat. Goals develop our instinct to never give up and to try again and again until we succeed. The Try Again instinct is linked to optimism. For someone to accomplish great things, they have to visualize success. They must believe that each time they try, their goal is just around the corner. Whether employee, business partner, child, or spouse, developing and nurturing this instinct, despite massive failure, makes a world of difference. This instinct is so important because fear consumes us and has the power to dictate everything in our lives. Think about it. We fear not falling in love—we find love, and we fear losing it. We fear not being successful—we find success, and we fear losing it. We fear not growing a family—we grow a family, and we fear losing it to death and unforeseen circumstances. Instead, let the fear drive you in a positive way—to be resilient and keep you accountable—to never give in to the fear but rather use it as a catapult to keep trying.

THE PROVE-IT-TO-ME INSTINCT

This instinct is about fact-finding and due diligence. It allows humans to let go of emotion and personal bias when analyzing new ideas and opportunities for the best outcome. This instinct is often suppressed as we're told to follow the rules and are discouraged from questioning the status quo. You see this in schools where students are asked to perform at a basic comprehension level, regurgitating information rather than researching, analyzing, and applying. In business, venture capitalists use this highly evolved skill to constantly assess how a business model will work, scale, and succeed without being distracted by excitement over the deal. For employees, this is about discovery with the allowance to question, analyze, and look at all outcomes.

The sooner someone strengthens this instinct, the sooner they will feel in control of their experiences and empowered to grow. To me, this is where the magic happens because once this instinct is ignited and the power to seek out and discover is flexed, you will never be the same. You will naturally start to do this in all things, and it will empower you to have a voice and be confident in your competence on what you are doing or speaking about.

THE I'LL-FIX-IT INSTINCT

This instinct is about seeing problems and the potential solutions to those problems. The ability to see new opportunities in everyday life while traveling, shopping, or working is at the heart of valuable entrepreneurial ideas and successful business models. It's essential to encourage both your children and your employees to "see a need, fill a need" so they gain the confidence which allows them to problem-solve and handle any situation.

This instinct is also a hero's instinct—that person who comes to the rescue in all situations or that person everyone thinks to call on for any crisis. My husband wrote the book on this instinct and leads his life with it in mind! I will share more about him later.

THE EVOLVING INSTINCT

The Evolving instinct is about being willing to change and evolve through what is not serving you. It requires extreme emotion to be removed from thinking about people, patterns, and processes that are not helping you succeed.

Understanding that the right path naturally eventuates, if you're willing to recognize it and take it, is one of the hardest instincts to develop. It is also one of the most important behavioral traits that help humans survive mental, emotional, physical, personal, and professional times of crisis. Throughout this journey, don't be afraid of people leaving you; worry about staying around when it no longer serves you. Matt and I have had many challenges in business, but we have sharpened this instinct because of crisis—mostly professional— and the people we are today would crush who we started out as. Throughout our journey and into today, we've managed to really develop and strengthen this instinct, and it has become one of our most vital tools.

THE WHATEVER-IT-TAKES INSTINCT

Working hard and sacrificing for what you really want to achieve is what this instinct is about. It's different than the Try-Again instinct because it requires out-of-the-box thinking. If something is not working, out of reach, unavailable, unfair, or unjust, humans have to make choices: "live with it in despair" or "do whatever it takes" to change it. Especially in school, children whose learning styles are not considered or catered to will either figure out how to learn "despite" challenges, or they will struggle without grasping the knowledge. We see this with employees as well. Often, they will just quit instead of doing what it takes to get the knowledge to succeed in their position. The problem with "quitting before learning" is that employees miss out on their own potential many times. In business, those "overnight successes" usually require at least five years of hard work and incredible sacrifice to get there and make the difference between staying in business or failing. All around us, people are looking for the "easy" button, the quick fix, or the secret to getting to millionaire status. Maybe it's a step-by-step guide to raising kids or all the answers in a single cheat sheet because they don't even want to invest in reading the book. This is not success in life; this is barely living. This instinct requires discipline and laser focus. Mastering this instinct will teach you to never negotiate your goals.

> If something is not working, out of reach, unavailable, unfair, or unjust, humans have to make choices: "live with it in despair" or "do whatever it takes" to change it.

THE GO-OUT-ON-A-LEDGE INSTINCT

This instinct is about "no risk, no reward." It's a fundamental factor of almost any major endeavor when we are young or when we are in business. There is a balance between risk and opportunity, and it is vital to understand when finding out what makes another human light up. This instinct develops stronger and faster in humans who are made to feel that failure is not bad but, rather, a necessary learning moment before success. I believe one of the biggest contributing factors to our success is, we always go out on a ledge. We never allow fear to stop the momentum. Most people starve between the idea and execution, but this has never been a problem for us. We don't recklessly jump, but we never pause long enough to stall out. Make sense? If you are one of those people who needs reassurance, you need to seek out a mentor because you could be standing in your own way of greatness.

Never negotiate your goals.

THE CONNECTIONS INSTINCT

This instinct is about connecting, communicating, and relationship building by developing a constant awareness that every point of communication matters because connections lead to opportunity; you develop the ability to sell your ideas to others. Whether communicating with partners, investors, vendors, employees, or children, every communication is an opportunity to strengthen your connection. Great communication is about selling others on the value of a relationship with you. To me, this is the all-around most important instinct in life. As you begin to understand the immense value in honing this instinct and helping the people in your orbit do the same, you will dive into other areas that are critical, like listening properly, reading body language, engagement, and retention. These skills will help you in all areas, from hiring new employees to solving issues with your spouse. The No. 1 lesson I teach my children is vital in business and life: Focus on relationships.

NURTURING ENTREPRENEURIAL INSTINCTS

When all humans, but especially kids, look within and identify these entrepreneurial instincts, they find that personal ambitions and goals rapidly materialize, progress, and improve. Courage, curiosity, confidence, and conviction are what turn sparks into fireworks. Understanding what drives kids and makes them think and act differently, or what might make them appear "weird" to others, allows them to view themselves as part of an extraordinary universe of individuals that think like them. This self-actualization frees them to create entirely new worlds of thought, play, and progress during their time on this planet because when humans understand why they do what they do, they feel included, not isolated.

Courage, curiosity, confidence, and conviction are what turn sparks into fireworks.

Human beings are so multifaceted, and no one is made up of a "single-story." When you take a moment to really absorb this thought, you can easily see that the same applies to your employees. I'm not telling you to treat your employees like children, but rather, give them the opportunity and tools needed to navigate their lives the same way.

YOUR ENTREPRENEURIAL CHILD

Helping your children start a business, no matter how small—regardless of their school situation—is an experience that will simultaneously stimulate the development of their entrepreneurial instincts and help them develop courage, curiosity, confidence, and conviction. Listen and encourage them. Help them see the potential in their ideas or look for solutions to the problems that they see. Explain how to create a plan and the steps to take to execute the plan. Do they need investment? Structure a loan with interest and take this as an opportunity to introduce debt and payment plans. Encourage them to seek out investors in their orbit that they can present their plan.

A SPARK: JAXSON AND HIS WHEELS

Our son, Jaxson, is a great example of this. He loves to ride anything with wheels! He has a skateboard, rollerblades, hoverboard, and scooter, but he really likes to ride a bike. Unfortunately, he left his bike and gear outside one day, and it went missing. He understood that we wouldn't just go buy him another bike; he was responsible for the care of it, and he neglected to follow through. He desperately wanted a new bike. He ended up in a store one day getting something with his dad, and they passed the bike section. He asked if they could look and see the prices. He wanted to figure out how he could buy one.

They looked at the bikes and the prices, and he realized a few things. One, all the fancy gear shifting equaled a higher price. Two, he analyzed what he really needed from a bike. He asked his dad if he could take out a loan to buy the bike he'd pick out. Matt, seeing this as a great opportunity to teach him about debt, payments, interest, and the need to make money, said, "Sure, but you have to tell me how you will pay it back." They thought about the things that meant something to Jaxson, and they came up with a plan for him to start a recycling company. Matt taught him how to structure a loan and what interest is, but the deal was, he had to make his first payment in a week. That was a busy week! He solicited employees and friends to give him their recyclables. He went with his dad and found a business partner that he could deliver the recycling and get paid for it. Jaxson worked very hard to make sure he made a payment every week until his loan was paid off, and he owned his bike completely. It took him 10 weeks. Now he runs his business so he can buy his own gifts for people, save some money, and even invests in making his own interest. Making interest is his favorite part!

It has also become our daughter Bella's favorite part! How many times have you been somewhere and needed cash? Kids love having cash and tend to take it with them—at least mine do. We would always (and still do) turn to Bella and ask her if we could borrow cash for things like parking or for tipping for the luggage guy. We taught her about loans and interest at a young age, so she would lend us the money—$10, $20—and she would charge 10% interest. She loved the interest!!! She learned from about age 5 on how to calculate interest and how loans worked. It's a simple way to get your children thinking about money in a positive way.

IT'S NEVER TOO LATE TO SPARK

Imagine helping your business team develop courage, curiosity, confidence, and conviction. The 4 Big Cs. How would this shift in thinking change the scale and profit of your business? What if an employee came to you with the idea that transformed your company OR with a new business idea that you could partner on? In fact, when I hire, I look for these types of individuals and have had massive success and growth because we hire with this mindset. I also believe that we have to nudge the people we put on our team to help them see the areas that they have not tapped into but are peeking through to shine. However, I don't believe in hiring to strictly get as much as we can out of a person. It's more about how we combine their skills with the team and make incredible things happen. It's also about helping them use their time to acquire and master new skills and grow so they can move up in our organization or leave as a stronger human.

A great example of this is a hire we made a few months ago. This gentleman was hired to do multiple things, and really, he was picked because of his eagerness to learn and grow. His excitement to become a part of our team was infectious, and he came in ready to go! He has come to us with several solutions to cut down processing time and labor-intensive tasks, and he continues to innovate and create fresh ideas. Since he was hired with the growth culture and growth mindset in mind, we benefited tremendously. We could have easily put someone in his position, which was more qualified or had previous experience, but you can see how being open to other factors can lead to massive benefits. Humans are capable of incredible things—no matter our age. By understanding the 9 entrepreneurial Instincts we all possess, how to encourage their development into behavioral traits, and how to fuel a growth mindset in the people around us, we are helping ignite Firework Humans at every age.

Humans are capable of incredible things—no matter our age.

For additional resources, go to my website, JessicaMead.com, for even more information so you can put this into action. Just use the passcode StillOrbiting to get into the Member Section.

CHAPTER 6

Review & Reflect

REVIEW:

1. When all humans, but especially kids, look within and identify these entrepreneurial instincts, they find that personal ambitions and goals rapidly materialize, progress, and improve.

2. Helping your children start a business, no matter how small, is an experience that will stimulate the development of their entrepreneurial instincts and help them develop courage, curiosity, confidence, and conviction.

3. By understanding the 9 entrepreneurial Instincts we all possess, how to encourage their development into behavioral traits, and how to fuel a growth mindset in the people around us, we are helping ignite Firework Humans at every age.

REFLECT:

1. Thinking about the 9 entrepreneurial Instincts, which ones do you feel strong in? Which ones could use some strengthening?

2. Thinking of your children or members of your leadership team, which instincts could you nurture?

3. Imagine helping your business team develop courage, curiosity, confidence, and conviction. How would this shift in thinking change the scale and profit of your business?

PART 2

THE 9 ENTREPRENEURIAL INSTINCTS

At the beginning of this book, I encouraged you to allow yourself to be transformed. I hope you found nuggets—big and small—that will help you on your path to becoming free to be and to helping those in your orbit—namely, your children, partner, or employees—on their journeys to becoming Firework Humans.

In the next few chapters, I'll detail how to recognize and nurture the 9 Entrepreneurial Instincts. Some people will develop certain instincts into behavioral traits and leave others undeveloped. Others will actively work to develop all of them at the same time, while others still continue to grow throughout their entire lives. No right. No wrong. It all depends on if they have someone championing their success. I'm also throwing in a bonus chapter on Learning Styles in this Part. It's another critical piece for both the growth mindset and entrepreneurial instincts.

CHAPTER 7

How to Nurture the Knowledge-Seeking Instinct

"Turns out, it's less about 'teaching' creativity—and more about creating a fertile environment in which their imagination will take root, grow, and flourish."

– Mitch Resnick, Director of Lifelong Kindergarten Group at MIT

THE KNOWLEDGE-SEEKING INSTINCT

I believe there is a misconception about learning and knowledge. Namely, something clicks at age 5 or 6 when children go to school, which is when the knowledge-seeking kicks in. Once high school or college is completed, education is over, and it's time to "be an adult" and produce. We chose to perpetuate this cycle of life for ourselves and our children. It is a choice to break this cycle and understand this fact: Humans are natural-born learners on a constant learning and knowledge journey. In fact, from their first breath, humans begin to observe and gain knowledge in a continuous process throughout their entire life. If they have an underdeveloped instinct around education and being excited about knowledge-seeking, it's not hard to spot.

I'm sure you've worked with people who don't believe they can solve problems on their own—it's costly and frustrating—especially since they don't have to feel that way. Whether you're a parent, a business owner, or both, encouraging someone, who thinks they have limitations, exceed those perceived limits, is one of the most rewarding experiences you'll ever have. It is vital that we guide all humans toward discovering solutions for themselves. They need to feel the rush of success pulse through their own veins and see the results with their own eyes. Only then will they put forth the effort to continue solving problems and expanding their minds. There is a powerful way that we, as the authority figure in their lives, can set them up to learn, grow, and flourish. But first, we must start with ourselves. I talk to myself to motivate and encourage, to show mercy and understanding when I can't quite get it together.

> **It is vital that we guide all humans toward discovering solutions for themselves.**

Once I understood that I had the power to shift my mind and realize everything is bendable, I became the architect of my life. I became the author and the voice dictating my story and my life plan. Then, I became fearless to lead, help, educate, encourage, and be someone who could do the same for others.

Here are some signs to watch for with your kids:

1. Do they struggle to get their homework done?
2. Are they struggling to do well in school?
3. Do they need prodding to ask questions?
4. Is it difficult to communicate with them?
5. Do they display a lack of engagement?
6. Do they speak of being bored?
7. Is anxiety a problem around school issues?
8. Is their social group small or tenuous?
9. Are they complaining that they are learning useless information?
10. Do they avoid reading for fun?
11. Do they question why things are happening?

Here are some signs to watch for with your employees:

1. Do they struggle to meet deadlines?
2. Do they speak up and ask questions in meetings?
3. Are they proactive problem solvers?

4. Do they perform well as part of a team?
5. Do they speak of being overwhelmed with work?
6. Is anxiety a problem?
7. Do they complain that they don't understand specific systems or rules?
8. Do they avoid company enrichment activities like webinars or recommended reading?
9. Do they question why things are happening?

Watching out for these signs will help you know that you might need to nurture the Knowledge-Seeking instinct.

BOOSTING THE UNDER-DEVELOPED INSTINCT

Research from the Grattan Institute[6] reports that about 40% of school students claim to be regularly unproductive, bored, or struggling to keep up in school. In other words, four out of ten kids have an under-developed Knowledge-Seeking instinct. Whether you choose to homeschool or stay the traditional course, you as a parent can mentor and strengthen your child's ability to instinctually love learning.

The way I see it with employees, it can be 50/50. While children learn how to evolve their instincts into behavioral traits, adults have already either developed—or left dormant—these same instincts. If they have a fixed mindset, it may be tough to nurture their courage, curiosity, confidence, and conviction. It's essential to be honest with employees about the culture you're trying to establish and clarify that knowledge-seeking is a core value. Employees with a fixed mindset who are unwilling to evolve will weed themselves out.

It starts by working on this lack of engagement at home and in the workspace. One way to do it is by asking your children questions about what they learned, so they have a chance to be proud of their newfound Knowledge—letting them teach you something new. (This also works great with members of your work team). Allowing your kids to guide you will help develop your skills to become a great teacher. With employees, ask them to teach you how they approach their tasks or communicate with clients. Challenge them to gain that knowledge in the areas that catapult them to the next level in their current position or get to the place they desire. Then, make sure to follow up and engage in that knowledge quest.

INTEREST-BASED LEARNING

Interest-based learning is a key to this instinct—in fact, it is a magic sauce of sorts for our family. Have them read books on topics they are interested in—even if it is a comic book—or create lessons around whatever that interest is. Connect learning to fun and value creation (the second component of entrepreneurial behavior I spoke of in Chapter 6). Become interested in what they are focused on and ask questions about it. Then, start asking questions about what they seem disinterested in. Show them you are curious about their views.

For example, ask your child these questions:
1. In Math, "How can you use that in real life?"
2. In Science, "Do you think that has new uses in today's world?"
3. In English, "Who would be a modern-day equivalent of that character?"
4. In their interest, "Tell me why you think I should get into that comic book? What's cool about it?"

Your questions, and their answers, need to be age-appropriate—but you'll find they get excited about their ability to answer them and will often exceed your expectations! Learning is a lifelong journey, and "school" is not a punishment but instead is a way to do concentrated learning. It's important to point out to your child all the ways they are learning so they see it happening in all situations, not just in the classroom. Look for things that can create a struggle, like social issues or emotional issues, such as anxiety or potential learning disorders. Kids are natural over-compensators, so you'll have to get them to identify their problems in ways that make them feel safe and unashamed. You can also look into learning assessments to discover their learning style and create a plan around how they best take in information (See Chapter 5.) Figuring this out is one of the things I believe is vital to a fruitful and positive educational journey.

Sample questions to ask your child:
1. What was your favorite part of school today, and why?

2.   What was your least favorite part, and why?
3.   What was the hardest thing you did today, and why?
4.   What was one thing you wish you could have changed that happened today?

With your employees—or other adults in your life—it's also essential to look at the areas where they struggle. If you know they have a growth mindset, then nurturing their Knowledge-Seeking instinct will be received more quickly than if they have a fixed mindset.

Sample questions to ask your employee:
1.   What was your favorite part of the workweek, and why?
2.   What was your least favorite part, and why?
3.   What was the hardest thing you did for a client, and why?
4.   What was one thing you wish you could have changed that happened this week?

The best way to stimulate the Knowledge-Seeking instinct is to make learning fun! It can be as simple for young kids as making counting games with their toys or getting them to try to spell words from their favorite books. For older kids, help them discover their passions and interests and encourage them to pursue them both in and out of school. Don't judge or worry about what they want to learn about or practice. If they are enjoying the learning process, they develop their instinct, which will make them lifelong learners. If their learning style is not lining up with their learning plan, then you have an opportunity to change it before they become disenchanted.

The goal is to make learning relevant. In particular, teenagers can get frustrated by what they think is having to learn "useless" or "irrelevant" information. But for every teen who has said, "Why do I need to learn this, anyway" is an adult who has said, "I wish I paid more attention to that in high school." For adults, making learning fun and enjoyable might include learning how to play a new game, take up a new hobby, or learn a new language. It might be traveling to a new place and experiencing new

Be sure to recognize achievements and reward accomplishments.

cultures. It might also be learning a new skill that will allow them to advance in their job or change careers to something they are passionate about. Always—always—encourage this! Also, be sure to recognize achievements and reward accomplishments. It might be as simple as acknowledging a team meeting or a congratulatory text to a friend. They could even "reward themselves" by inviting friends over to enjoy a meal they just learned to cook.

For your employees, set aside time every month (or week) for deliberate learning. Maybe it's an hour a week or 3 hours a month, but it's work time set aside to better themselves and enhance their skills. Have your leadership team host a lunch and update them on changes, or explain areas they may need clarity on, or do a Q&A session. It could also be making sure they attend conferences, workshops, or outside classes at some point during the year. Investing in human growth always pays off.

Focus on the Process, Not the Result

This is important, so I'm shouting this out for those of you in the back!

Students are under increasing pressure to get good grades, impeding their ability to perform well. You want to reduce the school's anxiety so it does not lead to an avoidance of going to class, homework, and studying. Anxiety surrounding performance takes the fun out of learning. Take the pressure off! A note about your employees and learning new things: you need to understand their learning styles (see Chapter 17) and their background so you can provide training in a meaningful way. Maybe some of them learn by watching a video and studying a workbook, while others need live instruction, and yet others need to just do it until they figure it out. CEOs who ignore team learning styles risk undervaluing or losing a great employee because 1) how training is administered doesn't bring out their great traits, or 2) how ideas flourish with individual learning styles are often restricted. Meanwhile, a less dedicated and impactful employee gets the boost in position or pay because they are, what I call, a "good test taker." It's essential to see your team as individual humans with their own possibilities—just like with your children.

Punishing them or giving them a hard time for their poor results will make them dread the learning process.

COACH 'EM UP OR COACH 'EM OUT—YOU DECIDE

Instead of punishing your children or your employees, offer support—both emotionally and academically. Let them be open about their disappointments without fear of your judgment. And talk with them, listen to them, and collaborate to find ways that can help them improve and enjoy the process of learning, whether in a classroom, online or at home.

To help strengthen your child's Knowledge-Seeking instinct, you must lead by example. Talk often, ask questions, share stories, and seek out knowledge with them.

1. Read all kinds of books to and with young children—even with your preteens and young adults.
2. Discuss news stories and current events with your teenagers.
3. Have conversations around topical news events and industry news with your team.
4. Engage in a healthy debate!
5. Make the love of learning a daily activity in your home and office.

CHAPTER 7

REVIEW & REFLECT

REVIEW:

1. Humans are natural-born learners on a constant learning and knowledge journey.
2. The best way to stimulate the Knowledge-Seeking instinct is to make learning fun and relevant.
3. For your employees, set aside time every month (or week) for deliberate learning. Investing in human growth always pays off.

REFLECT:

1. What two or three things can you do with your children to help nurture their Knowledge-Seeking instinct?
2. What can you do with your team or employees to encourage them to want to continue to learn and grow?
3. How can you best lead your children or employees by example when it comes to continually learning and growing?

CHAPTER 8

How to Nurture the
Audacious Dreamer Instinct

THE AUDACIOUS DREAMER INSTINCT

Humans are born with so many different talents and massive potential for creating new things. If they have an underdeveloped instinct around connecting to their passions and how to dream bigger, you can see this clearly as a parent.

Here are some signs to watch for:
- Do they actively play every day?
- Do they do the bare minimum when given a creative school project?
- Are they shy when it comes to role-playing?
- Do they read books for fun?
- When talking with them, do they use adjectives to describe things?
- Do they speak of being bored if they are not using electronics?
- Do they tinker?
- Do they struggle to entertain themselves?
- Are they careful to speak their mind?
- Do they have trouble sticking up for themselves?
- Is their answer to any question, "I don't know," or "I don't care," or "Whatever you think"?
- The research conducted by The National Academy of Science in 2017[7] around a study in cognitive flexibility across human life history

from childhood to adolescence to adulthood helps explain why it is essential for children to strengthen their Audacious Dreamer instinct. The extensive study reveals exciting commentary on the topic.

- One specific point suggests that as learners grow older and have more experience, they become less sensitive to new evidence and more reliant on their prior beliefs.
- K-12 children are similar to each other and less flexible than preschoolers.
- Adolescents and adults are similar, and both are remarkably less flexible than preschoolers and school-aged children.

In other words, with age and life experiences, a creative mind can become less open to exploring new ideas. Why is this true? One of the critical things to look for in your business is burning out. Pay attention to your employees. When you see mistakes happening or lack of engagement, you can assume they are also losing that Audacious Dreamer instinct. Help get them back to a healthy place in their work environment—often, it's a matter of helping in one area to address an entirely different one. Things compound for adults, mainly because they let it happen, and the result is you see not one but several areas that start to crumble. As the leader, it's our job to watch for signs and create a path to a healthier place.

With age and life experiences, a creative mind can become less open to exploring new ideas.

My son has a hyper-developed Audacious Dreamer instinct that is so strong; it has become a trait in everything he does from performing, creating art, communicating—even how he dresses. He is always dreaming, ideating, creating, and solving problems. Had I put him in a traditional school setting not equipped to handle his learning style (see Chapter 17), I know he would have been marked as "the problem child" and would not have developed his Knowledge-Seeking and Audacious Dreamer instincts so strongly. Watching his mind work is one of the coolest things to witness! Giving him the freedom to travel through an art project or science experiment that flows into a full discovery of something new is one of the immense rewards for me. I get the same feeling when I talk to an employee through an issue—allowing them to give me all the ideas that their imagination creates to solve it. See, we can instruct, grant directives, and make the people in our lives follow our plan; but why would we when the beauty lies in allowing them to flourish, create, and grow. Every single human can lead their life this way. It is the conditioning through authority and life's challenges that make this part of them die.

The three big things to consider here are:
1. The environment your child or employee is in.
2. How well it's working for them.
3. How to encourage vulnerability is a virtue of the young.

"Saving face" is not important when you're younger. As a result, children don't mind asking "stupid" questions or suggesting crazy ideas. They don't care if their ideas are possibly unrealistic or dumb. They just immediately move on to the next idea. As we get older, and especially in the corporate environment, we become much more guarded. There's a great Ted Talk by Tom Wujec, called "The Marshmallow Challenge,"[8] that explores the research supporting this concept.

The Marshmallow Challenge is simple enough: Small teams have to build a structure in 18 minutes using 20 sticks of spaghetti, 1 yard of tape, 1 yard of string, and 1 marshmallow. The winning team constructs the tallest, freestanding structure with the marshmallow on top within the time allowed. The point is to collaborate very quickly to finish the task. The results are fascinating and speak to many ways business leaders need to change company culture. As it relates to raising children with vulnerability, the results speak volumes.

WHO PERFORMS POORLY?

Recent business school graduates. They try to find the single correct way to do it. They cheat. Get distracted. They run out of time, and when they put the marshmallow on top, it's a crisis.

WHO PERFORMS WELL?

Kindergarteners. None of the kids spend time trying to become CEO of the Marshmallow Challenge. They start with the marshmallow and then build successive prototypes, all the time keeping the marshmallow on top until they find a way that works. Kindergarteners prototype and refine. They adopt an iterative, collaborative process and get instant feedback on what does and doesn't work. They don't naturally feel ashamed if their ideas don't work. They try new ideas instead.

Unfortunately, the vulnerability that allows them to experiment with new ideas (key for creativity) disappears as they grow up and start working in big corporations. Any environment where mistakes are not tolerated—school or companies—has adverse consequences for the humans they serve; they stop wanting to try new things because of the possibility of failure and how their peers might exploit it. As students move up in grades past kindergarten, they have behavior and processing expectations placed on them that start to develop this adult mentality that is crippling as they grow. But it doesn't have to be this way!

This single concept is one of the main reasons I chose to homeschool my kids from K-12. I can foster their ability to be vulnerable by providing an environment that stimulates creativity, trial and error, and no fear of ridicule. I try to create a similar environment for my employees. I show them that I am just as vulnerable and looking for an opportunity to learn from them the same way they are looking to learn from me. Therefore, in meetings or conversations, I make sure I pause to ask if anyone has questions or thoughts, sometimes even throwing one out there that I feel might be one, but no one is courageous enough to ask. I do this for people to "rescue" them for the sake of ridicule or fear and show them that if I am willing, they should feel empowered.

> Any environment where mistakes are not tolerated has adverse consequences for the humans they serve; they stop wanting to try new things because of the possibility of failure.

I've found that this alone has allowed many people in my orbit to let go and have a voice. People, this is such a gift and if we all could take off the mask and be vulnerable and willing to fail, we show others that it's going to be okay. As a leader, I see this as one of the best gifts I can give. That's why you will find me making goofy faces, not shying away from belting out a tune off-key, dancing down the hallways, delivering terrible jokes, and especially, being okay with embarrassment. I can do this because my Audacious Dreamer instinct allows me to do whatever and be whatever my heart feels good about. Inside each of us is the power to shift the "feel of a room" or change the course of a conversation, redirect to an imaginative and open place for creativity. Sadly, we hold back for fear of being exposed—that maybe we sound silly or dumb. I will tell you that the magic happens when you are willing to invest in yourself and your dreams.

AUDACIOUS DREAMER INSTINCTS

Another way to develop the Audacious Dreamer instinct is to treat your child as if they were a budding businessperson. This is not to say you are trying to push your child into business; it's quite the opposite. You might know that earmuffs, popsicles, and the trampoline were kid-innovations. Berkshire Hathaway CEO Warren Buffett, who is worth billions, began hustling as a child, going door to door selling chewing gum. (My husband did something similar!)

Children can come up with some pretty unique ideas when you let them play. They are sponges, and you can teach them how to innovate their ideas by linking them to results. Dreaming up ways to make money and trying to do it as young as possible helps your child develop necessary life skills while simultaneously teaching them valuable financial lessons. Even if they fail at making money with their ideas, the process itself is invaluable. It helps them learn perseverance and critical thinking about money, communication, negotiation skills, and even vision building. Adding a "build your own business" course to your child's education journey is a must, and you are qualified to do it. Have them build a lemonade stand, start an Etsy store, or design an APP. Having them birth an idea, develop it, and try to make money doing it will show them how to turn dreams into tangible, sometimes life-changing, realities.

> The magic happens when you are willing to invest in yourself and your dreams.

I think it's important to help the people in our orbit see how they can visualize or see their dreams. To think bigger! I know people who set daily goals to get to their big goal, others build vision boards, others use self-talk and affirmations, some start to live as though they have already achieved it. Regardless of the method you use, be willing to share that with others so they can see it in action. Showing people in your orbit that it's okay to allow themselves to do this and believe in themselves is a gift that keeps giving. It gets them thinking and excited about life and the possibilities they still possess. I use a vision board, self-talk, and live as though I have achieved my goal. I believe it because I believe in myself.

CHAPTER 8

REVIEW & REFLECT

REVIEW:

1. Audacious Dreamers are always dreaming, ideating, creating, and solving problems.
2. The Audacious Dreamer instinct allows you to do whatever and be whatever your heart feels good about. Inside each of us is the power to redirect to an imaginative and open place for creativity.
3. It's important to help the people in our orbit see how they can visualize their dreams and to think bigger!

REFLECT:

1. Are you an Audacious Dreamer? How would you rate your ability to dream big and accomplish your goals?
2. In what ways can you nurture this instinct with your children?
3. How can you help your employees feel safe to dream big?

CHAPTER 9

How to Nurture the Try-Again Instinct

THE TRY-AGAIN INSTINCT

Humans who develop resiliency have an easier time in the face of obstacles, including bullying, moving, divorce, anxiety, and other life events that pop up. If they view failure as a negative, it's essential to identify it quickly and flip the switch.

These are signs of an underdeveloped Try-Again Instinct:
1. Do they have coping issues?
2. Do they take risks?
3. Will a sudden change in their world cause them to become upset?
4. Have they been bullied and changed their openness to meeting new people?
5. Are they overly emotional or not emotional enough?
6. Do they have challenges around staying positive?
7. Are they not curious about "why" things happen?
8. Do they struggle to entertain themselves?
9. Do they suffer from anxiety?
10. Do they spend a good majority of their time inside?

RESILIENCY – THE BACKBONE OF THE TRY-AGAIN INSTINCT

Resilience is the ability to push through stress, adversity, failure, challenges, or even trauma and then bounce back. It's about trying again until you get it right and not being afraid of taking a risk because you might fail. All humans are born resilient (think about what babies goes through at birth and even the first few months of their lives!), and we can develop strong resiliency, but we have to work at it. As entrepreneurs with a growth mindset, "finding a way despite" results from our strongly developed Try-Again instinct. Everyone encounters stress as they grow up and as they grow as humans. Parents try, but ultimately, they can't protect kids from illness, bullying, divorce, losing friends, grief, or any number of traumatic events that can or have happened throughout childhood.

Resilient humans take risks because they know they can get back up after they've been knocked down. They share traits like curiosity and bravery. They are not afraid to get out of their comfort zones and are trusting of their instincts. This leads them to solve problems independently. Whether that describes your child or your ideal employee, it is something to strive toward continuously. This instinct has much to do with the ability to develop courage, curiosity, confidence, and conviction.

> **Resilient humans take risks because they know they can get back up after they've been knocked down.**

So, how do you encourage this in your child or your employees? Let me share with you something that recently happened at BrandLync. We lost a client group that has been with my President and VP of Automotive for a long time. So long that they were more friends than anything else, they both took this as a big blow. I found out right before our weekly meeting on Friday, where we do a weekly recap and plan, to move into the next week. I could see the defeat on their faces; from their body language to how they talked, it was a living presence in the atmosphere. (Mind you, we are on Zoom.) I could see it added to the TODO section of the meeting agenda, and when the time came to tell the group and talk about it, my stomach was a wreck for these two guys.

I listened and allowed the defeat to rush out. Heads were down, and you could see how hard it was to deliver this news. When they finished, I asked to speak first. I said, "I see that this has physically and mentally upset you both, and it's okay to wear it hard. But what I need you to understand is that I see this as a positive thing. I think this client group was an anchor tied to your ankles that were holding you back. This allows us to reset what we want to do for our customers rather than how we have always done it. Let's use this as a catapult to where we want to go."

I knew that something of this magnitude could break even the strongest humans and the brightest minds. I needed to remind them of how resilient they are and how to use this as ammunition for growth. And let me tell you— have they ever done it! We never felt the loss, and since then, they have both come back and said, "You were right. It was holding us back." Sometimes we need events to happen in our lives to remind us that we all have this trait—this resiliency—that lies within us.

WAYS TO NURTURE THE TRY-AGAIN INSTINCT

Let Them Figure It Out

Allowing people of all ages to solve their problems independently builds resilience. It helps them confront uncertainty and develop a skill set around getting through anxiety and adversity. Let them make the decision, and if they struggle, break the decision down and show them how each option can be a good one. So many adults cannot make a single decision without struggling and having anxiety over it. Encourage this needed skill early on. Empower your children to decide personal things for themselves—like their hair, clothes, music, etc. We could easily tell our children (and employees) what to do, how to do it, what makes sense, but instead, putting it back on them is a gift they don't even know they need. I do this with work problems all the time. Rather than giving a team member the solution, I will say, "What do you think is the direction we should go?" or "What are three possible outcomes that you envision here?" Empowering people of all ages to become better decision-makers is vital to having a growth mindset and developing entrepreneurial instincts.

> Empowering people of all ages to become better decision-makers is vital to having a growth mindset and developing entrepreneurial instincts.

Let Them Take a Risk

When people avoid risk, they begin to internalize the message that they aren't strong enough to handle challenges. Push your child to go outside of their comfort zone in ways that will result in very little harm if they are unsuccessful. Examples include trying a new activity, participating in a school club, or striking up a conversation with the grocery store's cashier.

Taking risks equals being open to opportunity. The Spring of 2016 turned out to be one of the biggest periods in my professional life where I needed this resiliency, this try-it again, this pick yourself up and figure it out to carry me through. Let me explain. First, I have to rewind and drop us in mid-2014. We had our data company humming along and had the opportunity to pick up a small sales company out of Florida that was selling a similar, yet inferior, product to the one we had created. As we evaluated the deal over the next couple of months, they started leaning heavily on my husband for help—so much so that I said they either start paying for the time or we needed to buy their company. They realized the value Matt added, and he realized it was worth doing, so we acquired part of the company.

After meeting them, I quickly had reservations—my intuition was waving all sorts of red flags. The value they brought to the table was not real, and so we ultimately settled on a larger stake in the company in exchange for our staying involved. I bowed out and didn't have any part of that company. They loved having Matt at the helm. He rebuilt the entire company from the inside out. He recreated, developed, and advanced the products and services which led to massive growth—working tirelessly through weekends and vacations to do so. As we explored an additional acquisition, we went looking for a CEO to run that company if we decided to close on it. Little did we realize that this person we let into our orbit would become a player in this game—he saw the success Matt was creating at the previous company and wanted a part of it.

When we decided not to close on the project we originally recruited him for (because my intuition told me no), I wouldn't give him any part of the companies Matt and I had built together. So, we isolated the relationship in a separate entity. (In hindsight, this was a brilliant move and exceptional instinct on my part.) The company started growing, and, before long, the immense jealousy from the minority partners over mine and Matt's overall success kicked into high gear. The two original guys and the new one worked together and colluded to push Matt out of the company and created chaos across the entire organization. One day we are thriving, and the next, we are trying to figure out how to keep going and keep our team employed. They took everything, used game theory to make him feel like it was his fault, and it became very ugly. I'm sparing you lots of details, but to say we were devastated is an understatement. We had dozens of employees and went from millions to below zero and had to figure out how to keep everything going.

Every instinct inside of me kicked in, and I built a wall around Matt so that he could get his mind right, rebuild a new suite of products, and start all over. It was a very hard time in our professional life, and it crossed into our personal, but having that resiliency and strong desire to get back up and keep moving forward ultimately led to bigger success. What we thought was the worst thing to ever happen to us morphed into the best thing.

There are times in our lives when we will be tested, our integrity questioned, our grit and determination stretched, our emotions violated, and our will to carry on will fade. Being resilient will be the one thing that will slowly bring us back to ourselves.

There are several things you can do in the workplace to encourage your employees to take risks. I think the first and maybe most important one, is to lead by example. Demonstrate what it means to take a calculated risk and recover when it doesn't pay off. You can also define what a smart risk is. There are risks that only the owner of a company should be engaging in, but if you set the parameters around what an intelligent risk is, employees will feel safer about taking risks. Finally, reward risk-takers and never shame the risk-takers who fail. There's always something to be learned.

> There are times in our lives when we will be tested, our integrity questioned, and our grit and determination stretched. Being resilient will be the one thing that will slowly bring us back to ourselves.

Don't Fix It for Them

When kids or employees come to you to solve their problems, resist the natural response to fix it for them or give them the answer. Instead, ask questions and help them think through the solution. Make kids come up with their list of ideas with the pros and cons listed out. Make them think. By brainstorming solutions with kids, we engage them. With employees, it's essential to get them thinking about how to solve the problem themselves. As noted above, ask them questions to get them thinking about possible solutions. Before you know it, they will come to you, not only with the problem but also with suggestions for resolving it. Teach them how to live in the solution and not the problem.

Make Failing Okay

When parents focus only on end results, kids get caught up in the pass/fail cycle. They either succeed, or they don't. This causes risk avoidance and a fixed mindset. Being OKAY to make mistakes helps promote a growth mindset and gives kids the message that mistakes help them learn.

Failure is feedback.

In the workplace, define what failure is. While we typically think of loss as something that occurs when we don't meet goals or objectives, Sarah Blakely, CEO of Spanx, defines failure as merely "not trying" rather than focusing on the outcome. Also, promote the idea that failure is feedback. If something didn't work, it's a great chance to learn and try again with more knowledge. Lastly, I believe it's important to embrace failure. You might not fail when you choose the safe path, but you also miss out on the innovative ideas that come from falling.

Promote the Brightside—Every Experience Has One

Pessimism is a form of self-protection that can come from early childhood trauma like bullying or a harsh teacher or family hardship. Pessimism is the cousin of a fixed mindset, and often they play together in your child's mind. Some kids may appear more naturally optimistic than others, but optimism can be developed. If you have a mini pessimist on your hands, respect the feelings that lead to pessimistic thinking, and teach your child to reframe their thoughts to find the positive side. It's a process. In the workplace, help your resident pessimist to look for the possibilities, not the impossibilities. Focusing on the impossibilities promotes the fixed mindset that something can't be done and can be overwhelming. Promote the use of positive

Pessimism is the cousin of a fixed mindset, and often they play together in your child's mind.

language. Reframe negative situations as I did in the story above about losing a close client.

Get Physical Outside

Resilience to stress and adversity can be made stronger by regular exercise as it fuels the brain. All humans need time outdoors, engaging in physical activity. If team sports don't appeal to your children, encourage them to ride a bicycle, play tag, or go for walks. Teenagers can pick up a love for outdoor yoga or rollerblading. You can even make it a family affair! We like to take family walks or hike the hills in Encino, pair up and workout, swim, kayak together, and bike around the city of Seattle. Jaxson is in a constant state of physical activity; his mind craves it, and he thrives because of it.

Encourage your employees to take breaks to walk outside. Also, encourage them to walk to the local sandwich shop to get lunch rather than deliver. You can even go so far as providing membership to a health club as an employee benefit. The brain benefits from physical exercise, just like your muscles do. These are just a few of the numerous ways to foster the Try-Again instinct and help grow resiliency in the folks around you.

I want to make a special point about kids with anxiety issues. I have several friends whose children have anxiety conditions. It can be a struggle to find ways to create positive engagement where the child feels good about the activity rather than forced to be doing something. The BIG LESSON: it's "okay to not be successful" in *every* aspect of life. All kids have sparks of interest where the anxiety melts away to a certain extent allowing the connection, engagement, and risk-taking. Our job as parents is to nurture these instincts and activities to balance out the areas of life that create greater anxiety. For some of the children I mentioned, it's dance, music, playing an instrument, chess club, babysitting, and art. Often you will see that the child is an entirely different person when it comes to these interests, even engaging in activities that could be considered high anxiety.

On the flip side, I've met many children who seem to have no interests and fall into the isolation or anxiety category. When I meet these kids, I spend time talking to them, and within that conversation, I pull out a spark of interest by asking engaging questions. They contribute to the conversation freely and openly—talking about things that interest them but that they haven't had the opportunity to explore. If you have a child that suffers from anxiety, helping develop this instinct will make a huge difference. Kidshealth.org

The takeaway here is the more we push ourselves, our children, and employees beyond their paralyzing fear or anxiety, the louder and brighter the fireworks will become.

CHAPTER 9

Review & Reflect

Review:

1. Resilience—the ability to push through stress, adversity, failure, challenges, or even trauma, and then bounce back—is the key to the Try-Again instinct.
2. Allowing people of all ages to solve their problems independently builds resilience. It helps them confront uncertainty and develop a skill set around getting through anxiety and adversity.
3. When kids or employees come to you to solve their problems, resist the natural response to fix it for them or give them the answer. Instead, ask questions and help them think through the solution.

Reflect:

1. Think about your children or employees. Do they get right back up when knocked down?
2. What is one way you can help your children feel more empowered to make mistakes and try again?
3. What is one change you can make in your office that will help grow your employees' resilience?

CHAPTER 10

How to Nurture the Prove-It-to-Me Instinct

THE PROVE-IT-TO-ME INSTINCT

The Prove-It-to-Me instinct is all about critical thinking—the ability to engage in reflective and independent thinking. It is an active skill and one that generally requires the use of reasoning. Critical thinkers also ask numerous questions and rarely take things at face value. Historically, humans did not evolve by following the rules. Raising your child as a critical thinker with keen investigation abilities is directly connected to their happiness and success. How can you tell how developed someone's Prove-It-to-Me instinct is?

Here are some signs to watch for in children:

- Do they have a problem with authority?
- Are they a rule follower?
- Do they read books without being asked?
- Are they into Sci-Fi?
- Do they struggle with staying on a schedule?
- Are they good at playing alone?
- Are they frustrated by indirect answers to their questions?
- Do they always think they're "right?"
- Do they have a high IQ but trouble taking tests?

Here are some signs to watch for in your employees:

- Do they work independently?
- Do they find errors in their work or the work of others?
- Do they defend their mistakes?
- Do they take things at face value and move on?
- Do they question the status quo?
- Do they quickly jump to conclusions?

CRITICAL THINKING

The Foundation for Critical Thinking did a great interview with Linda Elder around critical thinking and gifted children.[9] This fascinating study covers a large amount of thought leadership and research around this topic. Two of the more significant points she made related to developing the **Prove-It-to-Me instinct** are the truth about intelligence and the lack of school-based programs teaching critical thinking to kids. The Center for Critical Thinking was asked to conduct a study for the California Commission on Teacher Credentialing[10] to determine the extent to which prospective teachers could teach critical thinking. It included randomly selected faculty from all private and public colleges and universities across California (including the University of California at Berkley and Stanford, as well as other prestigious higher education institutions).

The study showed that 89% of faculty considered critical thinking to be of primary importance, and only 19% could adequately articulate what critical thinking is. Also, more than 75% of those interviewed were unable to illustrate how to teach content around critical thinking.

The study concluded two significant things:

1. The fact that, as a rule, critical thinking is not presently being effectively taught at the high school and college/university level.
2. And yet, it is possible to do so.

WHY then, if it's possible to do so, don't more people do it? I have my suspicions. It's easier for teachers to lecture than it is to structure lessons around students, giving them the opportunity to develop their thoughts.

Teaching Critical Thinking

My best friend, Devon, who is a teacher, said to me, "Jessica, I went through high school and college and wished someone had pushed me to think more critically. It is such a vital skill. Even as a first-year teacher, it was difficult to implement it in my classroom. I wasn't taught how to execute on critical thinking in the classroom curriculum."

If you were to walk into any high school today, likely, you would not witness much critical thinking taking place. For too long, schools have relied on basic comprehension, memorization, and worksheet-based activities that involve very little cognitive demand. Sure, students are completing activities, but they are not necessarily learning and growing.

Most companies are no better. Systems are set up for accountability based on a pre-set way of doing things. When something fluctuates in business, employees are often stuck—not because they are not smart enough to figure out a new solution—but because they've been conditioned not to think outside of the company-approved system critically.

> Critical thinking is the most important—and most transferable— skill that we can teach humans.

Critical thinking is the most important— and most transferable—skill that we can teach humans. It gives them the ability to analyze a situation and plot multiple outcomes or solutions, make inferences about existing data, engage in deep reflection, and evaluate the effectiveness of a process. So why don't we nurture this valuable life skill? What will it take to help both children and adults alike become critical thinkers?

Well, many educators just don't know how. In fact, Devon was one of them. When she first started teaching, it seemed like an impossible feat to push her high school students to think. If they couldn't even correctly answer the comprehension questions, then how could they even begin with critical thinking?

The answer: modeling. Whether at home, school, work—or even sporting events and other activities—we learn best when someone first shows us how to think. (Notice that I didn't say *what* to think.) Comprehension-based activities occur most frequently in classrooms that view learning as a dutiful regurgitation of facts. Little gems memorized, tested, and ultimately forgotten.

In a high school English class, this could look like the difference between the following two questions:

1. Which phrase is a metaphor?
2. How does the metaphor develop the character?

Through modeling via whole-class discussion, a good teacher will think aloud: reading the text, pausing to note important details, and asking questions to guide students' attention toward the qualities the character exhibits. She may say, "This is an interesting detail. Why do you think the author would include this? What could it reveal about our character?" The teacher listens, annotates the text with ideas from the class, and pushes them to extend their thinking. By the time the class arrives at the metaphor, students are ready. By modeling the thinking skills necessary to answer question B, students can now break into smaller groups and work together to brainstorm possible answers.

A good teacher builds capacity in her students, giving them the confidence they need to tackle difficult tasks independently. A history teacher might ask the question, "Where did this battle take place?" This is a response that a student can easily put their finger on. They can literally point to the answer in the text. This type of basic comprehension question merely checks to see if a child completed the activity. It focuses on compliance rather than learning, and when teachers don't move beyond this type of questioning, students do not develop critical thinking skills. Imagine if the teacher followed up with the question, "Let's look up this location on Google Earth. Hmmm...why do you think they chose this particular spot?" While this question would likely be over many students' heads, with the appropriate level of teacher modeling and patience, students will learn to think critically. The best part of all of this is that we can do this in all areas of our life.

When you homeschool, you have control over your child's learning experiences. You can monitor their comprehension and then *extend* it as necessary. A trip to the grocery store can open a wealth of opportunities. Which eggs should we buy? Ok, why did you pick that one? I like your ideas; can you tell me more? Which details on the package made you choose this one? When you get home, your child can learn the difference between free-range, cage-free, pasture-raised, grass-fed, and organic. Why is the cost different? Which one is healthier and why? Your child learns to apply critical thinking skills that will ultimately help him become a more knowledgeable consumer.

In business, your employees need to answer basic questions about their job and your business. However, the follow-up questions that will lead you to greater success ultimately require higher-level thinking skills. They must analyze that data to determine what it means, how it impacts the business, how it relates to other areas of the business, and what it reveals about the end consumer.

If you provide opportunities for employees to work in groups, consider taking the time to model your thinking. You will be surprised by the uniqueness of their ideas and how they may even impact your own. Everyone can be taught to think critically, especially when they are taught to unlock those abilities. One of the biggest reasons to become the CEO of your child's learning journey is so you can supplement their education and customize it to their learning style. This may mean some type of homeschooling, or it could mean increasing their public or private school. In either scenario, teaching your child how to develop a robust Prove-It-to-Me instinct is vital.

THE PROVE-IT-TO-ME INSTINCT AND GIFTED CHILDREN

In his book, *IQ in Question: The Truth About Intelligence*,[11] Michael Howe focuses on the relationship between IQ and one's ability to function in life successfully. In a nutshell, he determined that variables other than IQ (such as schooling and socio-economic class) play a far more significant role than one's IQ test performance in determining success in life.

As far as I know, there is no evidence to suggest that "gifted" students end up functioning better than the average person in dealing with life's problems. This is where I believe helping your children strengthen their critical thinking comes in. They have an instinct around fact-finding, due diligence, and not accepting information just because it is given to them—so help them develop it.

Instinctually, gifted children are not the best rule followers, and they challenge authority, including you. Challenging authority is not a bad thing as there are ways to do it and create positive results. Gifted children tend to see themselves as equal to—or even superior to—the adults in charge of them.[12] I think they tend to respond based on experiences without consideration

> Variables other than IQ play a far more significant role than one's IQ test performance in determining success in life.

for hierarchy. They simply know they are right and have no regard for being perceived as offensive or stepping on someone's toes.

We have often experienced this with our daughter, Bella. She is highly intelligent and, based on testing, is considered gifted. Conversations with her could come across as rude or with an air of superiority, but after years of nurturing the Prove-It-to-Me instinct, she does not assume she is right. She researches and formulates her ideas, so when she engages with authority figures, she can do so knowing she is right and leaving the anxiety out of the discussion. On a positive note, as we've worked to nurture and refine this instinct, Bella has also learned patience, active listening, weighing her audience, adjusting her tone, and the importance of timing. So, while this instinct often creates problems for gifted kids, teaching these to a child early on will help in these situations. After all, communication and relationship-building skills are vital aspects of the Prove-It-to-Me instinct.

CRITICAL THINKING IN YOUR COMPANY

Hands down, critical thinking is essential in any business. When you have a team of critical thinkers, you're better able to find creative solutions to problems that might not be obvious at first glance. To nurture the Prove-It-to-Me instinct in employees who are not critical thinkers, you first must have a culture that promotes critical thinking. We do this in our companies by welcoming the tough questions and encouraging our employees to openly talk through ideas.

We also avoid jumping to conclusions by (again) asking questions and not overthinking possible solutions.

We also work with our staff to help them learn critical thinking skills. Here are a few of the things we do:

- **Ask simple questions.** Sometimes solutions are found in the basics.
- **Question basic assumptions.** After all, we all know that assuming only makes a donkey out of you and me.
- **Remind them to think for themselves.** Just because they found one source on the internet doesn't mean that it's right—or that they don't possess their own brilliant ideas.

Use Different Lenses

Fact-checking, due diligence, and not accepting information blindly is one of those empowering skills that will benefit children and adults alike throughout their lives. As mentioned before, it's more important than ever, in today's technology-connected world, that people know how to think for themselves, especially given what is considered "truth" simply because it was on the internet. Actively encourage those in your orbit to spot a flawed argument and recognize biases. The goal here should be to motivate humans to seek out supporting data to their belief, not just single layer information, but also question what they are told using logic, not emotion.[13]

You want to actively encourage them to spot a flawed argument and recognize biases, even biases they created themselves—confirmation bias. Confirmation bias can be a harmful and dangerous thing for every human being. And let's face it, our children are going to face enough adversaries throughout their life, so we don't want them to become their own worst enemy. Teaching kids (and employees) how to seek out evidence that supports their beliefs as well as to question them and to question what they see and read can help them become better problem solvers and decision-makers. [14]

Here's a situation that has happened to me numerous times in business. I will get a call, and it goes something like this:

Employee: "I wanted to bring you up to speed on where we are at with Ed over at Company ABC. I looked at all their reports, and we are doing great. I think they just don't know how to read the report, and they think they are behind. I already talked to Sam and Lily, and they agree that we should do this..."

Me: "What about Harris? Did you talk to him?"

Employee: "Well, Harris was busy, and..."

See what happened here? Would you accept this and move on? This is where knowing your employees come into play. In this case, the situation was only talked through with people who would align with the messenger. This is very common. Employees will seek out other employees or management they feel will align with their thoughts or side of the situation and avoid communicating with anyone who disagrees. Even if they discuss with someone who disagrees, they will leave that person out of the conversation upon delivery of the issue.

It is very easy to let this infect a company, and before you know it, it's out of control. Matt and I talk to our staff about looking through different lenses in every situation. Getting them to understand this and applying it is a little daunting at first, but once they see it and start to use it, you will know that you have given them a vital tool, not only in your company but in their life!

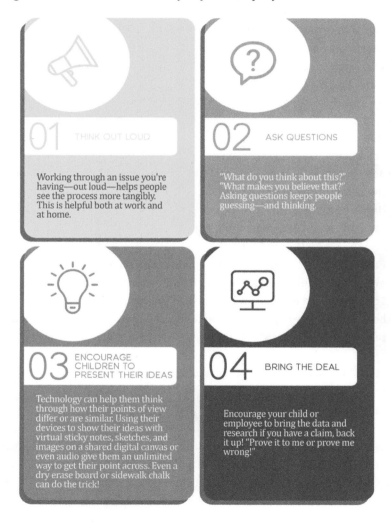

01 THINK OUT LOUD

Working through an issue you're having—out loud—helps people see the process more tangibly. This is helpful both at work and at home.

02 ASK QUESTIONS

"What do you think about this?" "What makes you believe that?" Asking questions keeps people guessing—and thinking.

03 ENCOURAGE CHILDREN TO PRESENT THEIR IDEAS

Technology can help them think through how their points of view differ or are similar. Using their devices to show their ideas with virtual sticky notes, sketches, and images on a shared digital canvas or even audio give them an unlimited way to get their point across. Even a dry erase board or sidewalk chalk can do the trick!

04 BRING THE DEAL

Encourage your child or employee to bring the data and research if you have a claim, back it up! "Prove it to me or prove me wrong!"

Remember, there is POWER in discovery and POWER in having the ability to FIND truth for YOURSELF! The sooner you start supporting this instinct, the better, as it helps feed the growth mindset more than any other instinct.

CHAPTER 10

REVIEW & REFLECT

REVIEW:

1. The Prove-It-to-Me instinct is all about critical thinking—the ability to engage in reflective and independent thinking. It is an active skill that generally requires the use of reasoning.

2. Children have an instinct around fact-finding, due diligence, and not accepting information just because it is given to them—so help them develop it.

3. Four ways to help evolve the Prove-It-to-Me instinct include: a) thinking out loud; b) asking questions; c) presenting ideas; d) bringing the data to prove their point.

REFLECT:

1. Think about your children or employees. Do you get frustrated when they ask numerous questions? When they won't accept the status quo? These are signs of their Prove-It-to-Me instinct. Be careful not to suppress it.

2. Actively encourage your children and your employees to spot a flawed argument and recognize biases.

3. What are three things you can do to nurture the Prove-It-to-Me instinct in your children or your employees?

CHAPTER 11

How to Nurture the I'll-Fix-It Instinct

THE I'LL-FIX-IT INSTINCT

Humans kept getting lost until someone in the Han Dynasty (China, 20 BC-20 AD) invented the compass. At its very root, need creates opportunity. Our human instinct to fix something is the most entrepreneurial trait that connects humans. But opportunities rarely present themselves on a silver platter. You have to look for them. The I'll-Fix-It instinct is about just that—finding those opportunities where something isn't working, is broken, is a pain point, or could be better—and then taking the initiative to fix it.

This instinct, I know after 20+ years in business, is about spotting opportunities disguised as problems that most people overlook. By strengthening this instinct until it becomes a strong behavior trait, you help your kids and employees become self-reliant forever.

> **This instinct is about spotting opportunities disguised as problems that most people overlook.**

Create the habit of what I call "opportunity spotting." Inspiring humans to develop their instincts around spotting opportunities starts by making sure they have options to fix problems. Sometimes, this requires breaking things for them to improve. Let me explain. Ever since I've had kids, I've wanted to nurture the entrepreneurial spirit inside them. I've experienced the freedom to think on my terms, the ability it grants to architect a fantastic lifestyle, and the many rewards that entrepreneurship can provide, so I focus on making sure Bella and Jaxson are exposed to it as much as possible.

Kids want to buy things. Employees wish to have certain things, as well. Some of those things naturally require saving up money and waiting until the budget frees up. I tell everyone in my orbit that there are opportunities everywhere to earn money. It's a matter of noticing problems and then finding— or creating—a solution to address those problems. One simple example is one I spotted when I was chatting with a lady at a Starbucks. We were talking about how many people are too busy to clean their houses well. However, many local companies were charging too much to clean customers' homes. This lady was so motivated by our conversation that she started an affordable cleaning company to solve these homeowners' issues and reach a broader audience. Everyone is happy. She spotted an opportunity and her Fix-It instinct kicked in.

As we all know, opportunities to solve problems in this world can come from unexpected places, so when you're trained to notice them, you're much more likely to benefit from these opportunities. Many times, when I'm out and about with my kiddos, I'll point out a business. I'll explain the problem that they are solving and how they are getting paid to do it. I don't force it down their throats (most kids hate that); I just casually discuss it when it comes up.

I let my kids know that if they see a mess around the house or outside, they should come to me to make a deal. They need to explain the issue and then make me an offer to correct the problem. When there are leaves in the pool, holiday decorations that need to be put away, or any task that is not part of our usual, all-hands-on-deck helping out, one of my kids may make an offer to take care of it. After a little negotiating—BAM! They get to make some extra money, and I get a few hours to do the things I need to do! It's as simple as that. I make clear that if I see the problem and then ask them to solve it, it doesn't count because they didn't find it on their own. That's what keeps humans always on the lookout. And, at this point, it has turned into a bit of a family game.

Another lesson they get with this is learning to negotiate. Negotiating skills are vital as an adult—having good negotiating skills and being brave enough to enact them can ensure success and help build better relationships. Not to mention, it can change every single interaction! Sometimes I counter their offer and go back and forth with them. We have fun with it, and the kids really get a kick out of negotiating.

Obviously, the problems they are solving at five years old are different than at 10, 15, and so on. Their ability to spot a problem evolves too. Starting kids out at an early age will put them way ahead on that learning curve. My favorite is when one of them comes to us with something, and they have thoroughly thought through and anticipated the negotiation ahead of time—super proud moment—and we are usually sold before the presentation is over! Bella goes so far as making PowerPoint presentations, complete with graphs and transitions!

This level of critical thinking is especially vital as our children grow and move into the adult world. They must be able to look at every situation—whether obstacle or opportunity—and calculate their next move. This is also a skill I work to foster in my employees by asking questions like, "Did you consider your time and its value when you put that SOW together for the client? Tell me what you think it's worth or how we should price it based on your knowledge of the scope of work involved?" I try to encourage them to be prepared, communicate, don't sell themselves or our company short, and think about the alternatives or other possibilities involved.

Jaxson wanted a new bike and wanted to be able to pick and buy anyone he wanted. He saw an opportunity to do this by starting a business in recycling. He first went and found a business partner who he could deliver the recycling to, and then he negotiated the rates with him based on volume and consistency. He got it up and making money, even soliciting our employees to collect recycling that he would pick up (selling them on the idea that, not only were they helping him achieve his goals but that it also has a positive impact it has on the earth!). Once he had the profits stacked up, he went and found the bike he wanted. He didn't have enough to pay for it, so he negotiated a loan and terms with interest. He did all of this at eight years old! Jaxson is incredibly proud and knows the value of his efforts and decisions through this experience. These are often small tasks for small amounts of money, but it gets them in the habit of having that "opportunity" instinct and keeps them always on the lookout.

THE I'LL-FIX-IT INSTINCT IN THE WORKPLACE

The growth mindset is essential to the I'll-Fix-It instinct. You have to be willing to open your eyes and not just spot a problem but then believe that you can provide a solution. I tell my team (and my kids) not to just come to me with problems. Please bring me a solution too. When they come with only a problem,

I get into a dialogue with them, asking them questions designed to get them to come up with the idea for solving it. It might not always be the best or most appropriate solution, but it's the first step in getting them to think about how to solve the issue creatively.

I implement this process at all my companies. I encourage the team to keep an eye out for problems or inefficiencies in the company, both inside and outside their role of responsibility and then bring me a plan to solve it along with how much it may cost to make it happen, in some cases paying them outside of their role to fix it. Typically, the solutions they come up with are right on because they know the company so well, and what they are asking for in return is well within the lines of reasons and less costly and time-sucking than hiring outside the company to complete this task. The team feels empowered for being able to "Fix It" as well as rewarded and encouraged for their solutions. In this way, they are always bringing me new ideas and solutions that make my companies more robust and more successful. It's a win-win.

Moreover, this self-reliant trait will carry on with them for the rest of their lives. Knowing that I am surrounding myself with humans with a strongly developed "I'll-Fix-It instinct" puts me at ease, knowing they'll make things happen from nothing. As Bella and Jaxson get older and become adults, they will capitalize on many opportunities that allow them to live a life on their terms instead of being forced into doing jobs they hate just for a paycheck. But when they do work for someone else, I promise you they will be the most valued employee, just like when one of my employees moves on, I'm positive their next company is getting a valuable asset in them.

I have yet to witness this instinct as strong in a person as I have in my husband, and it has led to massive success and relationship building. I would almost say that this is his strongest instinct, and he can't help but engage it in all aspects of his life. He is the fixer. If anyone is struggling or has a problem, either professional or personal, in their business or in a relationship, has a product that doesn't work or can't make sense of financials—it does not matter—he has this ability to see things through many lenses and can visualize paths or solutions no one can see. He is the first person people turn to, and I am both proud and grateful that he is this person for so many. Homing in on this one instinct can be rewarding both mentally and monetarily is an understatement.

Here's a great example. Our daughter, around the age of 13, saw the opportunity to replace our babysitter. So, she worked to prove to us she was responsible enough and able to assume the job herself! She started doing things like making meals for Jaxson, helping him with things his dad and I would normally do, explain all the emergency procedures, be diligent about safety, and other things to prove to us that she was ready and capable! She has been our babysitter for three-plus years. With the money she earns from watching her younger brother, she can purchase things she wants and save for future goals. She also gets paid to be an assistant to me—our kids are involved in our companies and know what we do and what it takes to accomplish this life we live. She started helping me with small tasks a few years ago, like notetaking or looking up information, and we realized she is fully capable and feels valuable in the process. Now she helps me daily with these tasks as well as many others.

CHAPTER 11

REVIEW & REFLECT

REVIEW:

1. The I'll-Fix-It instinct is about just that—finding those opportunities where something isn't working, is broken, is a pain point, or could be better—and then taking the initiative to fix it.
2. The growth mindset is essential to the I'll-Fix-It instinct. You have to be willing to open your eyes and not just spot a problem but then believe that you can provide a solution.
3. By strengthening this instinct until it becomes a strong behavior trait, you help your kids and employees become self-reliant.

REFLECT:

1. Think about your children/employees. Are they able to spot problems? What can you do to help them, not only spot them but find creative solutions to them?
2. What are one or two ways you can empower your employees and nurture their Fix-It instinct?
3. In what ways can you encourage your children to come to you with solutions?

CHAPTER 12

How to Nurture the Evolving Instinct

THE EVOLVING INSTINCT

As I'm writing this book, the entire world is involved with the COVID-19 pandemic, tumultuous elections, and civil unrest around the Black Lives Matter movement. Our kids—and our businesses—have been forced to evolve in many ways. From how they go to school and interact with people daily to handling fear of uncertainty and staying safe day-to-day, they must find new ways to do things. For some, change is difficult, stressful, and slow. For others with a more highly-developed Evolving instinct, change becomes fluid, and opportunities are acknowledged over roadblocks. Some form of distance learning is likely required for most families during the pandemic and will probably continue to be used by all types of schools for the foreseeable future. Nurturing your child's instinct to reimagine, pivot, and change their circumstances is a survival skill needed now more than ever. So, how do you do it?

DEVELOPING YOUR EVOLVING INSTINCT

First, minimize rules.

If you want your humans to follow a bunch of rules, then it's much more likely that, when the time comes to solve a problem, he or she will look at how it's been solved before and look to the conventional ways of doing it, as opposed to saying, "Well, how can I approach this? What other solutions haven't been tried before?"

I read a study that explored the benefits of rules on a child's potential to be creative[15]. It looked at the families of children rated among the most creative 5 percent in their school system with those who were not exceptionally creative. The parents of the so-called ordinary children had an average of six rules, like schedules for homework, bedtime, and structured play periods. Highly creative children had an average of less than one rule given by their parents, which translated into a tendency to place emphasis on moral values rather than on specific rules, according to Harvard psychologist Teresa Amabile.

As I mentioned earlier, my six siblings and I were homeless, on and off, until I was in high school. Rules were not plentiful in our family, so I never really had the "how should I do this" question in my head. I'd just adapt and evolve in any situation.

Second, reason with humans.

Getting humans to follow your rules is easier if you explain why it is a rule. Teach them to consider who the rule benefits and who it protects, even how the rule may be bendable. That can be easier than explaining why the law is as it is. Still, if you're interested in future evolution, you should take the time to reason with them. Help them think about the consequences of their actions for themselves and others.

It is also valuable to teach them to consider what could happen if everyone decided to break a rule or law. How would it change the world we live in? This is much more beneficial than simply saying, "No!" or "That's against policy." Children who evolve into creative adults tend to have a strong moral compass because they've been nurtured in some way to see concern for the consequences their actions have on others. At the same time, they're given plenty of autonomy to figure out how they want to live with those values.

THE EVOLVING INSTINCT AT WORK

The Evolving instinct is more critical now inside your company's walls than it has ever been before. It seems fairly evident that we live in a reactionary society. So, for myself and the management teams across all our companies, it's been vital to guide and educate our customers and staff through this time. It has been essential to encourage a mind shift from anxiety and fear to optimism and strength so that they can visualize moving forward. We needed to assure them that we could navigate through this if we corrected our outlook and didn't get stuck in the quicksand of doubt and fear. We had two options: stop and react in a scared way based on everyone else's response, or pivot and figure out how, as a company, we can best serve our clients to ensure they mitigate catastrophe for their company and brand.

Through this challenge, we have evolved into a tighter, more efficient, and innovative league of companies. We have worked relentlessly to develop strategies for our customers to survive and thrive through this. The coolest part was seeing that our employees not only responded to this atmosphere of evolution but seeing how it crossed over into their lives outside of work.

One of the critical things in a crisis is how you control your emotions and responses. As a leader of both your company and your household, you need to be aware of this. You won't believe the difference it makes when you have dozens of people looking to you for the solution. During times of crisis and uncertainty, this instinct will make all the difference, which is why it should be nurtured. Once you have done so, you can essentially crisis-proof your business and your life. The idea of change—or evolving—can trigger some strong emotions. Change is very hard and daunting at first, and along the way its stressful and messy, creating doubt and fear but on the other side it's a beautiful evolution and worth the discomfort. I know this from personal experience.

MY EVOLUTION STORIES

Looking back now, I realize that my entire youth was a constant evolution because I had no other choice. But I want to share my first evolution story that helped move me from childhood to adulthood. It takes us back to when I was in high school. I grew up in constant uncertainty, so I was conditioned to attach a negative/scared feeling about change. Finding something to cling to and ride into the future was my biggest goal in high school. I tried everything, from

FFA to French Club, to the theater, to the morning announcement show. I was determined to figure out where I would thrive, and by doing so, ensure that I would not live how I grew up. I realized I was really into the theater—both behind the scenes and in front. Musical theatre was the main extracurricular activity at my high school, and can I just say, singing is not my strong suit! But that was okay because I embraced all areas of theatre and decided I would make this my primary plan.

I also loved economics and the debates we would have in class, so I had that as my backup plan. My first conversation with a college counselor really threw me into despair. I wasn't enough of "this," didn't have enough of "that," and why did I think my plan would work? A slight panic set in, and I stopped seeing her. I made myself a spreadsheet of pros and cons and factored in my strengths and weaknesses, which made it worse. I started to doubt my plan. Something in that conversation made my mind tell my heart that I couldn't do it—that the reality of who I am at the core would stifle me and keep me from even auditioning to get into college. I questioned everything I had thought of and planned for years. I freaked out for a solid 2-3 months and eventually ended up on a long call with my grandma. We laughed and cried, and, more importantly, she just listened. She helped me realize that I didn't have to have the answers that day and that life is about self-discovery, self-awareness, and self-evolution. It's important that we are continually working toward a better version of ourselves, but it doesn't mean we have to have it all figured out and stick to that plan.

Life and circumstances, as well as who we are, will all evolve, and that's okay. See, I was trying to place that current version of me into the version of me I saw walking into college. They didn't line up, and it terrified me. My intuition told me and guided me to imagine my path, but I let my doubts cloud that vision. I had to ask myself, "Is THIS for me?" This is what we do—at all stages of our lives. We let the fear and anxiety win, and we never evolve. We adopt someone else's version of how our life should be, and we live that life. Needless to say, I overcame my fears, but as I look at the experience, I am grateful I went through it. It taught me early on that I write my story, I control my journey, and I am made to evolve.

At the beginning of my "adult" life—my second evolution story—I would have anxiety as we would start a company and get it humming along. But it wasn't starting that ignited this anxiety. I would get anxious once it was running smoothly—when we would get in a comfortable place. And, for the first ten years of my journey with Matt, my mind went like this: We would develop this idea, grow it into a business, have it running well, and then things would level out. We would settle in, and life would be good—no flux or things always up in the air. See, I hated being at that point, that pivotal point of not sure which direction to go, or which is the best plan, or having variables that made for huge life decisions. I was always waiting for life to "settle in." So, we would get a new business to the point of running smoothly—and I knew I was about to sabotage the very thing I was seeking. You see, the comfortable place I was starting to fall into triggered something—EVERY SINGLE TIME. I would go to Matt and say something to this effect: "Babe, look at where we are and what we have accomplished. I am so proud of you—so proud of us. But is this it? Is this the limit to our potential? If it is, I am okay. I can make this work and be happy here. But do we have more?"

Why would I knowingly turn life upside down again and march right back into that unknown—that flux I was so desperately trying to get out of? I would literally ask this out loud—WHY? And the answer was always there: my evolving instinct was on fire. It never stops. It has its own life inside me. Thankfully, I paired up with a man who was equally as strong, if not stronger! Wow, can we ever evolve and change—and our life together proves it. Now, he would get frustrated and do that typical guy thing, like "Is this not good enough?!" and "Why do we need to do more?" Here is the magic of this moment. I could see he wasn't done, that he had bigger things inside him. Watching his evolution is one of the most extraordinary experiences of my life.

I found peace from that anxiety about three years or so ago because a part of me still felt like, one day, we would find that place where we would stop and just "settle in." What I now know is that the word "settle" has no room in my vocabulary—that my make-up as a human being will never observe the meaning of "settle." AND THAT IS OKAY!

> The word "settle" has no room in my vocabulary.

CHAPTER 12

REVIEW & REFLECT

REVIEW:

1. Nurturing your child's (or employee's) instinct to reimagine, pivot, and change their circumstances is a survival skill needed now more than ever.
2. These two things will help develop your Evolving instinct: a) minimize rules; and b) reason with humans.
3. The idea of change—or evolving—can trigger some strong emotions, which, as a leader at home and in the office, need to be kept in check.

REFLECT:

1. When you find yourself in a crisis, do you rely on old methods for getting through the crisis, or do you look for new ways to handle the situation?
2. How do you feel when change is forced upon you from outside sources?
3. In what ways can you encourage your employees to embrace change?

CHAPTER 13

How to Nurture the Whatever-It-Takes Instinct

THE WHATEVER-IT-TAKES INSTINCT

This instinct is all about developing a strong work ethic. I'm sure you know the old expression, "actions speak louder than words." It's especially true when instilling a positive work ethic. Work ethic is built on strong character traits, like drive, determination, integrity, endurance, motivation, consistency, clarity, and confidence. By demonstrating it for both your children and your employees, you will model good work habits for them. The best way to teach critical thinking is to model it. It's the same way here. When your children or employees see you doing whatever it takes to accomplish the mission, it sets the example for what they should do. It inspires them to do better and be better than the current version of themselves.

> When your children or employees see you doing whatever it takes to accomplish the mission, it sets the example for what they should do.

I have a friend who was a single mom with one teenage daughter. She lived in a city that was a plane ride away from family. My friend knew she had no choice but to do whatever it took to make sure her daughter had what she needed, that she was able to homeschool her, and that her daughter was growing into an amazing young woman. She worked long hours and sacrificed (as many parents do) to provide a special life for the two of them. What she didn't realize at the time was that she was instilling in her daughter the work ethic of a strong, independent woman. Her daughter is now 22 years old, motivated, determined, living on her own, and loving life. She's one of the most valued employees at her company, not just because she works hard but because she's willing to do whatever it takes to help her team and her company succeed. She watched her momma and has a strong Whatever-It-Takes instinct that is still growing.

Don't ask anything of your children that you wouldn't do yourself. As you can see from above, they are paying attention! The same goes for when you are coaching or teaching your employees. Matt and I have always had a rule in business—we don't ask anything of our employees that we cannot or will not do ourselves, and it has served us well.

When Matt and I first got into business together, he wanted me on his one-man team, but I didn't really have any skills that benefited his business. I helped him with his books, but he really needed a designer to help him layout and design his publications in order to grow—he was doing everything himself. I would go with him at night to Kinkos, where he used the computers and printed proofs and things for customers. I would see these guys on the computers creating really cool things. Here's where my Whatever-It-Takes instinct kicked in! I started a conversation with one of the designers who was working on a project and asked if he could teach me his skills. In exchange for him sharing his knowledge, I paid for his computer time. I dedicated every night after work to gaining the skills I needed to fill the design role that Matt needed me to fill. This made all the difference for us as we grew. He was able to sell full-time while I created the layout and design for the publications. And just like that—BAM!—we were on the verge of our first million-dollar company.

This work ethic has followed us through every single business we've ever owned—from Matt learning how to cook in a professional kitchen for our restaurants, to running a printing press, to learning the wholesale market, to writing software, to building identity graphs and data sets—every single business—one of us or both of us learned how to do every single part of the business. If we didn't know how to do something, we educated ourselves. This year, across our companies, we have seen this instinct ignite in most of our employees—doing whatever it takes to keep moving forward. This type of culture is priceless, especially in times of crisis.

TIPS FOR INSTILLING THE WHATEVER-IT-TAKES INSTINCT AT HOME

Some children decide they are going to be a doctor at age three, and they never waiver. Others will change their career aspirations weekly. It doesn't matter. Just start the conversation early—habits are firmly rooted by the third grade, so the more you work on nurturing this instinct, the better. Give them tasks that should be attainable for their age and consistently enforce that they do them. Again, encourage them to start their own business. We all remember kids who had a lemonade stand, walked dogs, or mowed lawns for extra cash— these are all still good ideas. One quick note about doing chores: I don't give my kids an allowance for doing chores. Chores are mandatory tasks that the whole family pitches in to get done. They shouldn't be paid to engage in our family unit. We are a team. I also believe that an allowance creates the opportunity to attach negative emotions to money.

For example, if a child misbehaves, gets a bad grade, or doesn't put the toothpaste back correctly, parents often decrease or take away the allowance. From a very young age, this teaches a child that mistakes or negative behavior will always result in punishment of some sort instead of an opportunity to learn and grow from that mess up. I'm not saying there shouldn't be consequences for these actions; I just don't feel money should be attached to a negative emotion with a child. It sets them up for a bad relationship with money in the future.

Along with working for money, you should involve them in volunteer work. Hard work doesn't always get a paycheck. Many volunteer programs offer family programs where kids over a certain age can participate. Nursing homes, animal shelters, schools, zoos, and faith organizations often have family volunteer options.

Our family probably understands this better than most. Before my grandma passed away, we took care of her in our home for 3½ years after she had a stroke. Taking care of her was a lot of work and dedication. Still, it was the right thing to do, and our family became more empathetic, caring, and passionate about helping others. This "volunteer" work taught valuable lessons that were never attached to money.

Here is a big way to grow this instinct into a lifelong skill: When showing someone a new skill, be sure to encourage improvement, and be specific in your praise. Don't just say, "Good job." Tell them specifically what was good— what it was that you liked. Remember that children won't grasp the task as easily as you do, especially the first few times. Patience is key, and the world won't end if they don't do it just the way you want. Let your children know that it's okay not to be perfect.

TIPS FOR INSTILLING THIS WORK ETHIC IN YOUR EMPLOYEES

Let's face it. Not everyone has a fully developed Whatever-It-Takes instinct. Too many people have a Whatever-It-Takes-to-Get-By-For-Now attitude. For example, it happens every year or so that we'll hire an employee who seemed like the right fit but who turns out to have a "get-by-for-now" mentality. If you find yourself in a similar situation, find a way to show this employee that they have more to offer. Maybe it's their approach—many times, they resort to this mentality because they tend to procrastinate. If you try to correct it and they are still stuck, you might need to consider if this employee is healthy or hazardous for the team.

1

WORK ETHICS

Be a model by demonstrating your own work ethic.

2

FUTURE

Get your children talking about what they want to be when they grow up or what future goals they have. Talk to your employees about what their goals and what it will take to achieve them.

3

CHORES

Give your children age-appropriate chores.
Give employees challenging work assignments that push them.

4

ENTREPRENEURSHIP

As mentioned before, encourage your children to start their own "business."

5

VOLUNTEER

Involve your children in volunteer work. We even allow employees to volunteer and get work credit for it.

6

HAVE FUN

Make work fun and engaging—at all ages!

7

FAILURE IS OK

Teach that failure is okay and how failure helps you see new possibilities.

CHAPTER 13

REVIEW & REFLECT

REVIEW:

1. This instinct is all about developing a strong work ethic.
2. Don't ask anything of your children that you wouldn't do yourself. The same goes for when you are coaching or teaching your employees.
3. When your children or employees see you doing whatever it takes to accomplish the mission, it sets the example for what they should do. It inspires them to do better and be better than the current version of themselves.

REFLECT:

1. Are there areas—at work or at home—where you need to be a better model of what you expect?
2. In what ways can you make work (or learning for your children) fun and engaging?
3. What are two or three ways you can encourage your employees or children to do whatever it takes?

CHAPTER 14

How to Nurture
the Go-Out-on-a-Ledge Instinct

THE GO-OUT-ON-A-LEDGE INSTINCT

This instinct is about the phrase we have all heard—no risk, no reward. It's a fundamental factor of almost any major endeavor when we are young or in business. However, humans all have different levels of risk tolerance. Here are various ways to assess if your child or employee is a natural-born risk-taker or if this instinct needs to be further developed into a skill.

TRAITS OF A RISK-TAKER

- Refuses to accept "normal" or status quo
- Is motivated by purpose
- Focuses on solving problems for others or creating value for others
- Collaborates—the more talented the person, the more engaged they become with that person
- Executes an idea—alone or with a team

These traits may, at first, seem not to apply to children but rather only to businesspeople. But let's examine them for a moment. Does your child dress on their own terms, ask a million questions, or always look for the loophole? Do they get motivated to participate in activities if they can see the reward?

Do they look for ways to help their friends or teachers, sometimes even when it creates more work on them? Do they love to participate in group activities?

The traits are the same no matter what age—and understanding this when they are young helps develop risk-taking as a valuable skill later in business.

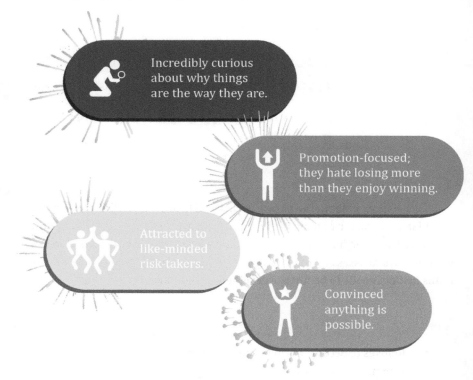

In Chapter 17, I will talk more about learning styles. Children with a highly-developed Go-Out-on-a-Ledge instinct often have very distinct learning styles. If these aren't acknowledged, it can lead to their disliking school, being labeled as problematic in some way, or simply checking out and going through the motions. It is essential to determine your child's risk-taking level as you decide on the education route that fits them best.

RISK-TAKING IN REAL LIFE

Our son, Jaxson, is a natural-born risk taker—the possibilities that lie within the "what-ifs" are way too enticing for him to pass up. As his personality developed, we knew early on that he would thrive and grow best in a homeschooling environment, but it would have to be shaped very differently than our daughter's. If he had gone to public or private school, he would have been labeled problematic, and his imagination would have been squashed. I'm not discrediting the school system but merely recognizing that he would constantly be challenging the norm with such a strong personality trait like Go-Out-on-a-Ledge. We have worked very hard to encourage this instinct because losing it would be a massive blow to his independence. It is part of his core foundation!

One of the biggest risks we watch Jaxson take is talking to people—he does this most of the time; if he sees a way, he can help them. For example, we were ice skating recently, and a mom and son were struggling—you could tell this was their first time, or they had not skated much in the past. He observed the struggle, and the next thing we knew, he was talking to them. Then he was showing them how to move. Then he was holding the boy's hand and guiding him. After 20-30 minutes, he had two more kids following him. Never did he consider the rejection that could happen; he only saw that he could help, and he was willing to try. The mom came up to us later and said how impressed she was and how kind our son was to her child. This happens all the time with him. He doesn't hesitate; he just does.

This is a hard one to nurture in adults/employees because the same fear and doubt kick in like they were actually standing on a ledge. Think about any physical situation you were in where you thought, what if I jump from this height into the lake? What if I jump from a plane, what if I...? These urges come in the form of excitement and high anxiety and then quickly recede as fast as they came. A part of you wants to experience the unknown, but the more prominent part of you says no way.

There were many lessons learned in 2020. BrandLync deals heavily in the automotive industry, and with all the shutdowns, we felt the strain of our client's closures like thousands of other businesses did. Not only did we have to reorganize our internal processes when they had to pause their marketing, but then we also had to help our clients think outside of their normal methods. This required us to think differently and not only be their marketing agency but also their business strategist in a rapidly changing environment. The process of doing this pushed us to evaluate our need to branch out and be in more verticals. This was something we had dabbled in but barely had our feet wet. Once we pulled the trigger and really focused on branching out, our team realized how truly incredible our programs and products are and the magic that they can do across all verticals. It also gave them fresh projects to work on, sparking new creativity. There is no secret here; we simply had to go out on a ledge and jump.

As a child, we don't quite yet understand the consequences. Although the examples I provide necessarily are not filled with negative consequences, we adults start to doubt them immediately. We have been conditioned to play it safe. We do this in our work as well. "What if I speak up and give them my idea?" "What if I ask for help?" "What if I told my boss I feel like I am drowning?" The same thing happens—we immediately shut it down for fear of looking inadequate or dumb, underqualified, or helpless. I have learned to recognize these signs—such as body language in a conversation, lack of engagement, an eagerness that quickly goes away. Now, keep in mind that these can be signs of other areas they may need help with, but communication is the key. Don't avoid these signs in hopes they will improve—communicate and address them right away.

There are several things you can do to encourage your employees to take a risk, including:

- *Lead by example.* Demonstrate what it means to take a calculated risk and how to recover when it doesn't pay off.
- *Define what a smart risk is.* If you set the parameters around what a smart risk is, then employees will feel safer about taking risks.
- *Reward risk-takers and never shame the risk-takers who fail.* There's always something to be learned.
- *Start small.* Encourage employees to proactively find little things that need correcting or improving and empower them to make those changes. You don't have to change the company in one fell swoop overnight. The little things add up.
- *Allow time to be creative.* Numerous discoveries and innovative ideas have come from employees being given time to just brainstorm—be creative and push boundaries. Countless features and products on Facebook were originally created during its hackathons, which gave engineers the chance to work on something not related to their day jobs.
- *Change the failure mindset.* I think getting employees to overcome their fear of failure is probably the biggest obstacle to tackle. You

can combat this by promoting the idea that there are learning opportunities when a risk doesn't pan out. Rather than disciplining someone whose idea failed, be sure to encourage them to share what was learned. This not only encourages the employee to keep taking risks, but when brainstorming with your team, you can uncover a solution that will become a success.

CHAPTER 14

Review & Reflect

REVIEW:

1. This instinct is all about risk-taking and learning how to take smart risks.
2. Risk takers are incredibly curious, promotion-focused, and convinced anything is possible.
3. This instinct is a hard one to nurture in adults/employees because the fear and doubt kick in like they were actually standing on a ledge.

REFLECT:

1. One of the best ways to nurture this instinct in your employees is to lead by example. Are you a risk-taker who is able to do this? What things can you do to best model these traits?
2. In what ways can you encourage your child to step out and take risks?
3. What two things can you implement at work to encourage risk-taking?

CHAPTER 15

How to Nurture the Connections Instinct

THE CONNECTIONS INSTINCT

Since the beginning of time, humans have needed to communicate and connect; by developing a constant awareness that every point of communication matters—because connection leads to opportunity—you develop the ability to sell your ideas to others. With this instinct, understanding why is as important as understanding how. Good communication skills are essential to success in all parts of our lives. Ask your teenager to take out the trash. Negotiate with the salesman for a new car. Call a housebound friend to say hello. Order take-out. Interview for a job. Run a meeting—this is just a fraction of the number of connections we make as humans.

> Good communication skills are essential to success in all parts of our lives.

We are social animals who need to connect with others on both a personal and business level for our well-being and, well, to get groceries. To be successful in making these vital connections, we must communicate our needs and expectations, and the more clearly, the better. Good communication is more than words. Your tone of voice, intention, what you leave out (and choose to put in), when you speak (and when you don't), and your body language all play a part in how your message is coming across—and affects your ability to connect. Want to get someone to have a closer relationship with you? Listen actively, watch your body language, ask questions, be clear and brief, clarify, reflect on what you have heard, be empathic, and be there and not mentally somewhere else.

Think about how many times you were turned off by how someone approached you. Was it their body language or word choice, or maybe it was via email or text, and it just felt off? Now think about how many times you engaged with someone but got nowhere, or they were curt in their response. Was it you? Was it them? It probably all came down to how you both communicate. I have witnessed million-dollar deals both fall apart and come to fruition, and it all came down to the communication taking place. In both scenarios, the numbers made sense—it was a fair deal—but understanding the art of communicating and executing on it effectively was the ultimate factor.

> I have witnessed million-dollar deals both fall apart and come to fruition, and it all came down to the communication taking place.

HELPING YOUR CHILD TO CONNECT

We learn to communicate from the moment we are born. The most basic things we do, like recognizing and feeding a hungry baby, asking a three-year-old what they are trying to say, making eye contact, or sitting down to read and cuddle, are the stepping stones and building blocks of communication skills. The individualization of homeschooling provides a unique opportunity to help your child become an effective communicator. Where else could you use role-playing to learn social communication or have the time to help a child learn correct word pronunciation?

It's important to remember that, especially for children, communication isn't just verbal. It's in our body language and writing. And if you think about it, most of education is either spoken or written, so if your child has issues with either one of these skills, it could create learning problems. The beauty of addressing communication skills in homeschool is that you can look at your children as individuals. You can help them learn through their preferred communication and grow in the areas where they struggle.

Whether you homeschool or not, you have the opportunity to help your children. Here are a few innovative ways you can further develop your child's communication skills.

Role-Playing

Role-playing or acting can help your child experience the feelings that come with communicating. This habit can be beneficial if your child has trouble reading social cues. Being able to experience how her words could affect others is valuable. My kids do improv as part of their homeschooling education and it has helped not only in communication but also creative thinking, engagement, concept integration, sharing ideas and bonding, active learning and confidence. It is also a good way to identify strengths and weaknesses. Improv classes are also great for adults!

Negotiating

When children learn to negotiate, it's just this incredible thing. They learn to be resourceful and develop their voice. And the coolest part of it is the confidence they gain; it's just a foregone conclusion in their mind that they will get their end goal. I encourage negotiating with your children throughout the day. It teaches them limits and possibilities.

Homeschooling allows children to be innovative, crafty, etc., in ways traditional education does not, especially in negotiations. And negotiating is a great way to enhance your communication skills and to practice connecting with someone else.

Watching and engaging in negotiations with my kiddos is one of my favorite things—they are tough! They have a voice, and they use it! Life is a negotiation, so learning this early on is a gift. It teaches them empathy, how to compromise, and builds self-esteem.

Negotiating is learning two sides of something. When we engage in negotiating with our children, we are giving them respect, independence, and power. That ultimately culminates in their becoming great decision-makers, and that is one of the most necessary things your child needs to walk away with. Their communication will improve, and they'll be better at developing relationships and communicating correctly and effectively with people.

EFFECTIVE CONNECTING SKILLS FOR ADULTS

As adults, the importance of good communication skills can't be overstated. When we communicate effectively, we engage others at a deeper level. In the workplace, this means greater understanding, increased productivity, and even a better work environment in general.

There are numerous techniques you can use to improve and enhance communication skills. Here are a few of my favorite ways that I find to be most effective.

- **Actively Listen** – This is more than just hearing; it's very intentional. It's setting the phone down, closing the lid on your computer, and giving the person speaking your undivided attention. Yes, this can be hard in this day of instant communication and the almost addictive need to see if we're needed and answer every ping that comes across our device. Maintain eye contact—don't be distracted by other things going on in your view. And ask for clarification, so there are no misunderstandings.
- **Really Listen and then Engage** – Don't listen for a moment and then zone out to figure out what to say to make a connection. Doing this and not listening and allowing that person to finish before you formulate a response keeps you from being actively engaged and hearing the whole message. Listen and let him/her finish, then respond—don't quit listening just so you can anticipate what to chime in with.
- **Body Language** – Watch yours and the person you're speaking with. What does your posture, eye contact, and facial expressions say about how receptive you are to be in this conversation? And what does the body language of the person you're speaking to say about how well they understand the message you're imparting? We are continually sending non-verbal cues whether we realize it or not, so be very intentional about what you're "not saying."
- **Take Notes** – Writing things down not only helps you after the conversation; it also shows the interest you're taking in what the other person is saying.
- **Brief but Specific** – Whether written or verbal, be sure to provide enough information for the other person to understand the message you're conveying without rambling on and on.

- **Think Before You Speak** – Take a moment to pay attention to what you're about to say. Doing so will save you headaches and heartaches in the long run.
- **Positivity** – Keep a smile on your face when you're on the phone. People can hear that positive attitude coming through the line and will respond more positively in return. Did you know that many call center agents keep a mirror in their workspace to remind them to smile? It does genuinely help to make that smile come through.
- **Be Mindful** – Teach them to be mindful of the words they choose to use in all interactions: choose positive and not negative.

When you have positive communication skills, you are better able to connect with others. Not only will you be more easily able to sell your products and services, but you can sell others on you and your ideas. People buy you!

Firework Humans might not be born with the best abilities to communicate, but these skills can be learned and honed. My communications skills have been a continuous work in progress throughout my life. Today, I will tell you that I believe it is my biggest strength, and it has served me well in my personal and professional life.

If there is one instinct I would say has the biggest potential to change your life, it is this one. Looking at the people in my orbit, if I could give them one thing, it would be to become better at connecting and communicating. I have witnessed massive shifts in courage, confidence, and consideration—in my employees, especially my leadership team—because we are constantly honing how we connect and communicate with our teams.

Encourage those in your orbit to sharpen these skills and watch their connections take off! Remember, there is a ripple effect in the efforts we make in other people. Helping them develop this skill will cross over into all areas of their lives.

> If there is one instinct that I would say has the biggest potential to change your life, it is the Connections instinct.

CHAPTER 15

REVIEW & REFLECT

REVIEW:

1. Humans need to communicate and connect. Being aware that every point of communication matters—because connection leads to opportunity—allows you to develop the ability to sell your ideas to others.

2. Two ways you can further develop your child's communication skills include role-playing and negotiating.

3. Good communication is more than words. Tone of voice, intention, what you leave out (and choose to put in), when you speak (and when you don't), and your body language all play a part in how your message is coming across—and affects your ability to connect.

REFLECT:

1. In what areas do you feel your communication skills are strong? What areas need strengthening? Be sure to take the time to improve your skills where needed.

2. Is your child a strong communicator (for his or her age)? What kind of role-playing can you do to help strengthen his or her skills?

3. Think about how your employees connect and communicate with each other and with your customers. What are two things you can do right away to help improve and grow effective communications skills?

CHAPTER 16

Examples of Firework Humans— The Famous, Young, and Impactful

Earlier, I talked about when we are young; we recognize little sparks of interest. We aren't quite sure what to do about them, but they turn into fireworks when those sparks are mentored. It's super-groovy that I have the opportunity to raise two children with the massive potential to become cool people that create fireworks throughout their life. It is the best gift I have been given. To see it through their actions and words, decisions and problem solving, communication, and relationships—it's pure magic! It's important to note that a child with strong entrepreneurial instincts and a growth mindset does not always grow up to be in business; they are musicians, artists, writers, philanthropists, and more. In fact, my kiddos fall in many of these categories, and my hope for them is that they try it all!

Let's first look at a few famous successful people who realized they were different and activated their Entrepreneurial Instincts. You'll notice they all have success in common, and, yes, they all have homeschooling in common. At the risk of being called biased, I will ask you to consider that there are no rules here. Humans can create their journey.

FAMOUS FIREWORK HUMANS

Simone Biles

In an interview with Great Homeschool Convention, Simone Biles[16] talked about how hard it was to leave public school for months at a time and how she spent a weekend in turmoil over her grandfather's decision to move her into a Christian homeschool experience at the age of 13. As it turns out, it would be the best decision for many reasons. The new academic freedom that homeschooling provided gave her 32 hours a week to train instead of the 20 hours she attended public school.

Simone won four gold medals and one bronze medal in the 2016 Olympics, putting her in the conversation as one of the greatest Olympic gymnasts ever. And with a combined total of 30 Olympic and World Championship medals, Biles is the most decorated American gymnast and the world's third most decorated gymnast. In future interviews, she admits that homeschooling was the only way to get serious about her training. Over her career, she has crushed stereotype after stereotype and opened up the thinking around homeschooling.

Christina Aguilera

The children at her Pennsylvania school bullied singer Christina Aguilera. In a CBS News interview, the former Mickey Mouse Club member said, "The bullying was so terrible that she dropped out of school in 9th grade and became a permanent homeschooler." Shortly after completing high school, Christina wrote "Reflection," a song for the Disney hit movie Mulan. She was also signed by RCA and released the first of many chart-topping, award-winning albums.

Suppose her mother had not recognized that she had the choice to allow Christina to evolve out of a negative situation. Would she have been able to become the success she is and has enjoyed such a long career?

Ryan Gosling

When Ryan Gosling was asked why he was homeschooled, he responded, "Because I was getting into a lot of trouble at school. I couldn't keep up. They were trying to put me in special ed classes. I remember I was playing chess in special ed, and I was playing against a kid who was eating his queen." At ten years old, he still couldn't read, was always getting into trouble at school, was diagnosed with Attention Deficit-Hyperactivity Disorder (ADHD), and was bullied.

Despite being a single mother, Ryan's mom decided to pull him out of school. Two years later, Disney's The Mickey Mouse Club gave him the first of many paid acting opportunities. Ryan told The Guardian that being homeschooled gave him "a sense of autonomy that I've never really lost." He is now one of the most successful actors in Hollywood.

Jan Koum

Jan Koum, the co-founder of WhatsApp, learned computer networking by himself with manuals from a used bookstore by 18. In 2009, Jan bought an iPhone, and his Audacious Dreamer and I'll-Fix-It instincts kicked in. He saw that apps would be the next big thing in technology and birthed an idea around creating a hassle-free and instant messaging service to get people worldwide to network on a single platform effortlessly. He tested different coding for months and used his Try-Again and Whatever-It-Takes instincts to bring WhatsApp into reality. Facebook later acquired it in February 2014 for $19.3 billion.

The exciting part of Jan's education story is that he attended a traditional high school in the U.S. after immigrating from Ukraine. He did well but was incredibly bored. His mother encouraged him to supplement his education by borrowing books and manuals and teaching himself a trade. He went to college but hated school and dropped out to co-found WhatsApp with Brian Acton.

HUMANS THAT SPARKED EARLY

Bill Gates might be one of the best-known young entrepreneurs we can point to, but it's happening more and more frequently. A Gallup Poll showed in late 2013 that 50% of minority students and 37% of white students in grades 5-12 were planning to start a business of their someday. This is phenomenal! And what's even more remarkable is the desire in these young people to give back to those in need. Imagine the world we could create if we had more young entrepreneurs!

Check out these young firework kidpreneurs!

In 2014, brothers Brandon and Sebastian Martinez (ages 14 and 12) started Are You Kidding Socks.[17] They help the Juvenile Diabetes Research Fund and Autism Speaks by selling funky-looking socks to schools for fundraisers.

In 2014, Alina Morse invested $7500 that her grandparents gave her for college into her own candy business called ZOLLIPOPS).[18] Since 2014, her candies have been available at SuperValu and Whole Foods along with Amazon. She has been tagged as the "Dentist's Best Friend" for her sugar-free treats.

In 2015, after identifying a child-sized gap in the travel market, Bella Tipping started Kidzcationz.com (https://kidzcationz.com/), a travel review website specifically for kids.

In 2016, Evan Moana started EvanTubeHD[19] and was named YouTube's youngest millionaire. He started this when he was in fourth grade. On his channel, he reviews toys and has more than 6 million subscribers. All the money Evan earns through sponsorships and advertisements is invested in college funds and investments for Evan and his sister, Jillian.

In 2017, 10-year-old Hannah Grace started BeYOUtiful).[20] You can find her products on her website, and she donates 20% of every purchase to the Juvenile Diabetes Research Fund, as she was diagnosed with Type 1 diabetes when she was an infant.

In 2018, Jelani Jones visited farmers' markets and tested as many products as she could find. One of those vendors became her mentor, and Jelani turned her bath product hobby into a lucrative career. She was 9 when she started her business and is now the "SheEO" of Lani Boo Bath.[21]

In 2019, David Holston launched his first entrepreneurial initiative when he made $35,000 in 4-days by posting an ad on Craigslist offering his truck for snow plowing during an unprecedented storm in Seattle. See a need, fill a need!

In 2020, Miracle Olatunji was named to BOSTINNO's Top 25 under 25.[22] She started OpportuniMe, an organization that provides personal and career development resources, opportunities, and content to the next generation of high school leaders. Last year, at age 19, she released her book, Purpose: How to Live and Lead with Impact. The miracle continues to work with OpportuniMe while attending Northeastern University.

That Gallup Poll wasn't kidding—these kidpreneurs are only a handful of the hundreds of businesses started by kids while they were still in school.

ANOTHER AMAZING FIREWORK HUMAN FROM MY WORLD

Now for one more example of a Firework Human from my world— my husband, business partner, father of our two kiddos, and an extreme visionary—Matt Mead. His education journey was fraught with labels about his learning abilities, and he was ultimately pulled out to homeschool. He struggled the entire time. He was a kid who processed and retained information in a completely different way than most kids. This is typically a challenge and disruption for most teachers (especially when they're young). It's easier to label and reprimand than embrace and encourage. His mind just saw things differently—and it still does.

He is the founder of several massively successful multimillion-dollar companies and has only begun to tap his potential. What gives? He harnessed and used his ability to solve problems, and his Fix-It instinct is second to none. He has evolved into this powerhouse of a man who can look at any product, situation, relationship, or company, see things you may never see, and help you make it go from broken or average to fixed and dynamic. The truth is that he was viewed as damaged and could have been written off, but his resiliency was so strong that he had no choice but to ride it to greatness. To say I am proud to stand next to him is an understatement!

For all of these examples, the initial sparks of curiosity and flexible mindset were encouraged and supported early on by parents in all sorts of life positions—and they became firework makers. Homeschooling, alternative education systems, and supplemental education can make the difference for kids and are not limited by a parent's professional responsibilities, educational background, or means.

Where there's a will, there's away.

CHAPTER 16

REVIEW & REFLECT

REVIEW:

1. A child with strong entrepreneurial instincts and a growth mindset does not always grow up to be in business; they are musicians, artists, writers, philanthropists, and more.

REFLECT:

1. Who, in your life, is a Firework Human? What qualities and traits do they have that make them the amazing Firework Human they are?

CHAPTER 17

UNDERSTANDING LEARNING STYLES

Intelligence is not a single thing but rather a modality of things. These things are learning styles. Understanding learning styles is also about understanding behavioral traits.

Have you observed your child and thought, I wish I could give him or her a better opportunity? A chance to just be themselves and learn in a new way? In a way that fits him, her, they, them exactly. If they got a reset, would they thrive in a new environment? What does "school" feel like in the absence of feeling peer pressure or being bullied? Do you, as a parent, want to create experiences for the family that are unique? Does letting your child grow in a natural way feel right? If you answered yes to any of these questions, homeschooling would be rewarding for your child. Homeschooling is another way that allows you and your child to dig deep and find out what their learning style is.

> Intelligence is not a single thing but rather a modality of things.

Parents consider it (and why many choose to do it) is because they connect directly with strengthening the 9 Entrepreneurial Instincts and promote a growth mindset directly or indirectly. I will debunk some of the myths and confirm some of the facts around all the different ways you can take charge of your child's learning journey. If homeschooling, understand that the only way to definitively know is to go through the process and just see what happens. I promise you won't "break" them. To do this effectively, you have to determine their learning styles. Once you have an understanding of learning styles, the rest will flow naturally.

HERE ARE EIGHT MAIN LEARNING STYLES

Now, you may be thinking that the idea of learning styles is outdated or debunked. You may even be wondering how this could even apply to you. We'll get there! I know people on both sides with strong opinions. But what I know for sure is that understanding what styles my children lean toward and work best with, arms me with the knowledge to better communicate and formulate their learning experience—which is valuable for all of us. The same holds true for my employees.

If you want to understand what type of learning style best suits you and how it may be the same or different for your children or employees, visit my website, JessicaMead.com, and take a self-assessment.

Many people only recognize four main learning styles: visual, auditory, logical, and kinesthetic. I lean towards recognizing eight main learning styles versus the four, and here is why.

I have witnessed bits of 3-4 learning styles in most human beings—with a predominant trait that guides the rest. Trying to use the main four that most recognize doesn't quite cover all the characteristics of learning, so we need to recognize the others.

Here they are:

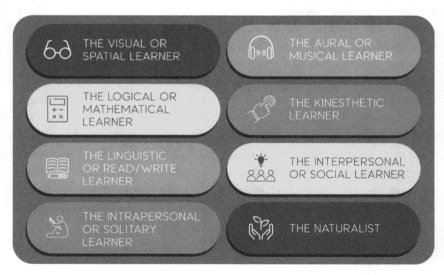

THE VISUAL OR SPATIAL LEARNER

THE AURAL OR MUSICAL LEARNER

THE LOGICAL OR MATHEMATICAL LEARNER

THE KINESTHETIC LEARNER

THE LINGUISTIC OR READ/WRITE LEARNER

THE INTERPERSONAL OR SOCIAL LEARNER

THE INTRAPERSONAL OR SOLITARY LEARNER

THE NATURALIST

DEFINING LEARNING STYLES

When trying to figure out your children's learning style, evaluate how theirs varies from yours and how you can then use strengths—yours and theirs—in a complementary way to help them learn at home. Use the same process with your employees. Let's look at the eight learning styles I believe are the most common in children and adults.

VISUAL LEARNER – THE "LET ME SEE IT" LEARNER

- Needs—and prefers—to visualize things, to see them written down on paper, on a whiteboard, or on a screen
- Learns by seeing—can easily remember the pictures they see on a page
- Usually, a fast talker and can be impatient
- Reads maps, charts, and diagrams with great competence
- Can sometimes be a daydreamer in class—especially if there's nothing to look at during a lesson
- Enjoys art and drawing
- Shows an interest in machines/inventions and how things work
- Enjoys playing with Legos/construction toys and likes to complete jigsaw puzzles

Ways to encourage this "Visual Learner" learning style:

- Use picture books of all types, even as they get older.
- Encourage writing by using different colors of writing.
- Teach "mind mapping" techniques to older children and employees to help them learn and recall complex information.
- Create visual patterns, play board games, and memory games.
- Use manipulatives in mathematics.
- Encourage visualization of a story and reinforce this at intervals.
- Show videos of plays, movies, etc., to reinforce the stories they are studying.

AUDITORY LEARNER – THE "LET ME HEAR IT" LEARNER

- Thinks in words (vs. pictures) and easily verbalizes concepts
- Tends to speak slower
- Good listener—prefers to listen and verbalize
- Linear thinker
- Spells words accurately and easily (they can hear the different sounds)
- Tends to learn spelling phonetically rather than through "look and say" techniques
- Has excellent memory, especially for names, dates, and trivia
- Likes word games
- Works best listening to music
- Often musically inclined, tapping rhythms, etc.

Ways to encourage this "Auditory Learner" learning style:
- Have your child read aloud and record the session for later playback.
- Have them create their own word problems.
- Audible books are fantastic for this learning style.
- Have them dictate a story and watch while you write or type it out.
- For older children, record certain lesson information so they can listen to it back, perhaps on their iPod.

LOGICAL LEARNER – THE "PUT IT IN ORDER" LEARNER

- Thinks conceptually and likes to explore patterns and relationships
- Likes to question everything and wonders about many things
- Likes routine and consistency
- Is easily able to do math in their head
- Enjoys strategy games, computers, and conducting experiments
- Likes having an end result to shoot for
- Enjoys puzzles and seeing how things work

- Likes to build things with blocks/Legos
- Not as competent when it comes to being creative
- Good at relationships

Ways to encourage this "Logical Learner" learning style:
- Include the use of computer learning games and word puzzles in your lessons.
- Conduct science experiments together.
- Introduce non-fiction and rhyming books.

KINESTHETIC LEARNER – THE "LET ME TOUCH IT" LEARNER

- Processes knowledge through touch and physical sensations
- Communicates using body language and gestures—talks with their hands a lot
- Very active, not able to sit still for a long time (and frequently misdiagnosed as ADD/ADHD)
- Would rather show you rather than tell you
- Prefers to experience the world around them by touching and feeling, making manipulatives key
- Often scientific in nature
- Enjoys sports or other activities that keep them moving

Ways to encourage this "Kinesthetic Learner" learning style:
- Allow children to move around every so often while studying—this movement helps them to focus.
- Incorporate hands-on activities and experiments, nature walks, art projects, or acting-out stories, so they "feel" the activities.
- Activities like doodling or fiddling with something—even chewing gum—can help them concentrate.
- Minimize the things they don't like, like long-range planning, complicated projects, paper & pencil tasks, and workbooks. These are restrictive to this type of learner.

THE LINGUISTIC OR READ/WRITE LEARNER:

- Prefers written text
- Learns best through words
- Enjoys reading and writing
- Note Writer
- Text is more powerful than any visual or auditory delivery of an idea

Ways to encourage this "Linguistic Learner" learning style:
- Retention is best when using textbooks, note-taking and verbalized lessons.
- This learning style caters to traditional education.
- Allow plenty of time to absorb the information and allow for comprehension.
- Give them written assignments.

THE INTERPERSONAL OR SOCIAL LEARNER:

- These are your team workers
- Creativity flourished in a group environment
- Excellent collaborators
- Storytellers
- Natural leaders
- This person learns by relating to others

Ways to encourage this "Interpersonal Learner" learning style:
- Put them on teams to work.
- Encourage collaboration.
- Give them opportunities to lead or "drive the bus" on new ideas.

THE INTRAPERSONAL OR SOLITARY LEARNER:

- Works best alone
- Solitary in nature
- Goal setters
- Self-driven with high self-management skills
- Very self-aware
- Independent
- Sometimes this person is an introvert
- Tends to become an entrepreneur—seeking a life that is not supervised

Ways to encourage this "Intrapersonal Learner" learning style:
- Allow space.
- Don't hover and trust their method.
- Give tools needed but allow self-driven learning.
- Don't force into group discussions or projects.

THE NATURALIST LEARNER:

- Keen observer of all things
- Wants to dig in and touch things, hold them
- Scientist
- Works best in nature and learning/experiencing through nature
- Hands-on experiences are key
- Experimentation equals knowledge
- Loves being outdoors
- Interest-based learner

Ways to encourage this "Naturalist Learner" learning style:
- Allow them to work outside as much as possible.
- Make as much of the learning hands-on or project-based.

- Manipulatives are encouraged to allow this learner to hold and see what they are learning about.
- Allow them to journal what they learn using charts, pictures and their thoughts.
- This learner will seek education and thrive best through interest-based learning.

A GUIDE FOR LEARNING STYLES

Learning styles were hot and heavy when the concept came about in the 80s and 90s. They were looked at very simply—if you're Audible, you can only learn by hearing. In my opinion, this misses the point of figuring out what a learning style truly is. Traditionally when you think of learning styles, you think of visual, auditory, tactile, and logical. These are too broad. Most people are a collection of these eight styles—not just one. My son, Jaxson, is an auditory learner, but he's also kinesthetic. He's also very social and a naturalist. Whereas my daughter Bella's defining factor is logic, she, however, is equally visual and auditory.

When you understand the concept of learning styles, you use a toolbox of different ways to help both children and adult learners think and execute. For example, with Bella, I had to create a "schoolhouse" when she was younger because one of her learning style preferences is to have structure. Even now that she is older, she does better and concentrates better, sitting at a desk and working. This is not unusual for her learning style preferences. No matter the size of your work area, you can create a learning space that best suits your child's needs. A counterexample would be Jaxson. He does not do well sitting at a desk or being confined to one area for an extended period of time. He can learn on the kitchen counter, the couch, the backyard, on the stairs— just not at a physical workstation. This is also not unusual for his learning style preferences.

> When you understand the concept of learning styles, you use a toolbox of different ways to help both children and adult learners think and execute.

You know your children and hopefully your employees well enough to tailor lessons or workshops to their style. If you start homeschooling when they're young, you're at a huge advantage because you already inherently understand their learning style. If you're pulling your child out of Jr. High, for example, there could be a bit of disconnect. You know the fundamentals, but you don't know the specifics of their learning style. No worries! You will just need to spend some time relearning it. Soon enough, you will know how to approach them to get the most out of them. You'll know when the right time is and what the right method will be. You can tell some children to do something, while others need the roundabout way of concluding that they need to do it without being told directly. Believe it or not, these are the same tactics that good classroom teachers use, but with anywhere from 20-200 total students per teacher, the chance is pretty high that at least one of your child's teachers will not be perceptive enough to determine your child's learning preferences.

Good employers also do this. For example, you may have two equally qualified employees performing the same tasks. One of them needs to be told exactly how to do something, including all the nuances and details. It's not because they are incapable of figuring the task out, but it's how they best learn and communicate. The second employee just needs to be told what the end result needs to be. To provide all the details of how to do it would only drive them nuts or make it more challenging to complete. They are equally qualified—equally valuable—they simply have different learning and communication styles.[23]

IDENTIFYING LEARNING STYLES

There are several online resources available to help you identify someone's learning style. A good one geared towards older kids and provides assessments for determining learning styles is Education Planner. There are also VARK (Visual, Auditory, Reading/Writing Preference, and Kinesthetic) tests out there to determine your learning style; however, these are aimed at older students and adults. When it comes to younger children, it's our job to watch them play and formulate an education plan based on observation and knowing our child—i.e., if your child constantly gets up and walks around, loves music and being outside, and does really well with a group versus solo work, you might think your child is a kinesthetic, aural learner who is social. The Social Learner's creativity flourishes in a group environment with natural leaders, and they learn by relating to others.

How does this help you? Well, you will not try and keep your child at a desk doing worksheets. Instead, plan the lesson based on his/her strengths. Take the class outside and make it into a group activity if possible. Now, you may be wondering how or why this matters when it comes to your business and employees? The answer here is simple: if you understand how your employees learn and you work toward those strengths and skills, you ensure success for your company. You know the best way to communicate and to engage, how they will contribute best, and by which method they will collaborate.

It is necessary to be aware of individual differences and accommodate them whenever possible. For example, I go into a meeting prepared to appeal to everyone's learning style so my visual learners can see it; my audio learners can hear it, etc. It's the same thing we do with our clients. We have taken the time to understand how they work best. By understanding this, we ensure our bond and their loyalty, and that creates sustainability and the opportunity to grow.[24]

> **If you understand how your employees learn and you work toward those strengths and skills, you ensure success for your company.**

DEVON ON LEARNING STYLES

Earlier, I introduced you to my friend, Devon, who shared some of her experiences as a high school teacher trying to teach critical thinking. She has some pretty brilliant ideas and observations. Here's another about learning styles.

"I was never that kind of kid that quickly thought up the right answer and victoriously threw my hand up into the air. And guess what? I'm not that adult either. It took me most of my adult life to realize that I am highly visual and kinesthetic. I must be able to create pictures in my mind and have the time and space to work with ideas physically. Chart paper is my best friend. I have exceptional analytical abilities. I can investigate a problem, determine all possible outcomes and start plotting ways to address each of them. However, when I'm in a room working with a team of extroverts, their constant verbal flow of ideas inhibits me from being able to do any of this. Instead of considering the multifaceted aspects of the project, they narrow in one aspect and just go with their first ideas. They repeat this process until they've 'finished.' Days later, they come back and notice that all of the separate, rushed ideas do not quite fit together, do not flow, and do not meet the end goal."

It is vital that we notice the learning and personality styles of our employees and pair them together accordingly. An introvert will go unheard in a room full of extroverts, despite the intensity and deep level of thought they can bring to the conversation. For each individual to become a Firework Human, they have to be able to share their voice, to be heard by others, and to develop that confidence to continue doing so. As leaders, it is our job to be intentional with our grouping for tasks.

Finding Materials

One final point about learning styles and your children. Different types of curriculum work better with different learning styles. If you want to learn about the different types of curriculum, check out my website, JessicaMead.com, for more information.

CHAPTER 17

REVIEW & REFLECT

REVIEW:

1. Understanding what learning styles your children and your employees lean toward and work best with arms you with the knowledge to better communicate and formulate their learning experience—which is valuable for all of us.
2. I believe there are eight learning styles. Humans tend to prefer 3-4 styles, with one predominant trait that guides the rest.
3. If you understand how your employees learn and you work toward those strengths and skills, you ensure success for your company. You know the best way to communicate and to engage, how they will contribute best, and by which method they will collaborate.

REFLECT:

1. What do you feel are your preferred learning styles? Which do you think is the dominant one?
2. Think about your children. Which learning styles do they favor?
3. Think about your employees. What things can you do to better adjust for their different learning styles and improve communication, training, meetings, etc.?

CHAPTER 18

Conclusion – My Vision for the Future

After reading through these pages, I hope that you have been able to envision a world filled with Firework Humans and what possibilities exist in that world. Whether I'm out shopping with my children or conducting a board meeting, I am always consciously looking for sparks in others. Rather than flame my passions and interests, I focused on igniting those in others. This mindset has allowed me to create an orbit where everyone around me feels open to dreaming, sharing, seeking, asking, and solving scenarios. Explosive things happen in my rotation because I have intentionally designed it that way.

I often say the phrase Still Orbiting. For me, this phrase is more like a mission. I have this dream. It's an entrepreneurial dream that I've nurtured since I was very young. It goes like this.

I walk into a ballroom. (Because I love a good party!)

There are hundreds of people present, standing in front of their chairs, clapping. The majority of these people are women, moms at large. They are clapping in support of the massive achievements of every human in that room. In this dream, the ballroom is filled with humans I encountered in a grocery line, on a plane, while buying a car, in a social media exchange, at the bank, or in a meeting at one of my companies. The meeting points are endless. Every human and I in this room have had a meaningful exchange, sometimes for just a few minutes and others over the years.

As I look around the room, I see humans who have come back from tragedy; others who have built a business from nothing while raising their children, others who have shifted from loathing their work to be passionate about expansion, and others still who have totally changed their entire life path even as old as 50, 60, or 70. Each of these humans will be clapping because they feel the fireworks inside themselves.

In this dream, we've all come together in this ballroom to celebrate the collaborative work we've done through the course of the year. We've helped ensure no kids go hungry at school, and those families have choices in how they educate their children, not tied to their economic advantages or lack of. We've all worked hard to make this happen through my non-profit, Mission E.A.T.

You see, for me, raising a phenomenal family, building a business empire, creating generational wealth, and traveling the world doing cool things, is not enough.

In my vision of a world with Firework Humans, I'm always looking for ways to create new opportunities for others.

Here are some of the ones I'm working on now:

1. **BrandLync** – my leading business venture is being scaled to $100M.
2. **Mission E.A.T.** – my non-profit with Matt around solving the hunger problem in schools and empowering families worldwide through education alternatives and financial literacy.
3. **Still Orbiting** – my live events seminar course where humans of all kinds can come and get the motivation, knowledge, and support to make the most of their trips around the sun.
4. **Kidpreneur Investing** – my program where kids pitch me a business idea and convince me to invest in their budding business at an early stage to mentor these instincts and business practices early in life.
5. **Angel Investing** – my portfolio of investments focused on supporting mothers in business.

Firework Humans is my first jump into the author's deep end. Is it perfect? No. And that's my advice to all Firework Humans. Don't wait for perfect and polished. Start creating explosions in all areas of your life. Start making every day count.

Do with passion,
refine with vision,
and always push the mission.

ACKNOWLEDGMENTS

This book—and, more so, the amazing life I get to live—would not be possible without the love and support of some remarkable humans!

Thank you to all the people in my life who have lifted me up, dragged me along, championed my dreams, ignored me enough to make me question myself, listened to me talk in "my book voice," stole my hours, followed me fearlessly, doubted my coolness, and ignited my sparks—you know who you are!

Matt, you are the greatest love this girl could ever hope for. You stimulate my mind and soul. You are a lover among legends, and I am so grateful I went to that pool party and smiled at you over Alonso's shoulder. Being your ride or die—second in command—partner in all things has made this life a thrill ride. Thank you for acknowledging and feeding my gypsy spirit, allowing me to lead us in my own weird and fearless way. This has allowed me to love with extreme intensity, follow my inner voice, and find great beauty and freedom in all I do. You are exactly what my heart yearned for, but...the songs you wrote and mix tapes you made are what really got me. You move me, and I will dance with you till the end.

P.S. Thanks for being the cocreator of our babies: MIC DROP!

Bella, your quick wit and sarcasm keep me going and make me cry and laugh all at the same time. You are the love that sparked growth and demanded me to be "more than." You have shown me life can be both immensely difficult and intensely beautiful at the same time, and when the world gets heavy, to stay soft. That all the pieces exist in every moment—it's just how we place them. You have taught me that love always come first. Your beautiful voice—when shared—captivates my heart and reminds me that not all things are freely given and are worth the wait. Through the harshest conditions, you are the soil that always blooms. BFF!

Jaxson, you are exactly what this family needed and have shown us what magic truly is. Your love and respect for the earth gives me great hope for the future. Quite honestly, your knowledge of all living things is mind-blowing, and you encourage or inspire everyone you meet. You always find a way to make

131

me think and see things in a different way—thank you for this. You have a way of reminding me to show up with an open heart and have made me a brave and intentional mama to you and your sister. Your BIG heart, deep emotional connection, focused dedication, and fearless determination in all you do is an inspiration to me every single day. You show all of us that helping others and kindness are exactly what is needed in most situations. Being silly with you is the key to life—I will wander with you forever.

Devon, you have the amazing ability to navigate my mind and have helped me put more of my soul into this book. You get me, I get you...we are each other's person.

Kristen, the mental housekeeping you provide me is unparalleled. You have a way of making the darkness beautiful. You are the world's greatest fake aunt and honorary sister!

Lindsey, for love lost and love found, our hearts finding each other again. We have survived many things and circled back when our souls needed it most.

Gigi and Uncle Kenny, you likely saved my life and set the foundation for who I am today. Thanks for caring for me and loving me.

Mom and Dad, a.k.a. Nana and Papaw, thank you for understanding my funky ways and accepting me for me. The unconditional love and support you always give is food for my gypsy spirit.

My employees throughout the years. You are what set me on this journey of discovery, understanding, and connection—this desire to inspire and educate. You have taught me how important it is to invest in people and help them as much as they help you—sometimes even more.

I also have to thank...

Brenda for always feeding my kids soup and Fernando the busboy at More Than Waffles. You have forever made me a better human being.

My dogs Geronimo Bleu and Ginger—you drive me insane but can cure my turmoil of emotions with a good lick on my face or in my ears. Kitty, a.k.a. Garfield Binx—your mood swings give me whiplash but...Yeah, I got nothing.

All the family pets who have died—you taught this family resiliency and how to ugly cry.

All the negative, miserable people in my life who were mean and unkind. Thanks for the negativity; it became my fuel to this extraordinary life!

The people who think they have gotten one over on me. Patience is my best virtue.

You are all the grooviest human beings on earth, and I am honored to be in your orbit!

Gratitude and Love,

ABOUT THE AUTHOR

In her 40 short years on this planet, Jessica has gone from homeless to leading lady and world changer. Her life has been one of self-reliance, and, in every way, non-traditional. "Self-reliance is in my DNA."

Growing up homeless on and off, sleeping in cars, motels, or a stranger's couch, Jessica often considered food with a question mark. Moving around constantly across three states, she was never in one place long enough for it to feel like home until her freshman year in high school. The oldest of seven, raised by parents who were constantly struggling and abusive in many ways, she naturally became the young caretaker of her family while she finished school.

Jessica met her future husband and business partner, Matt, while pursuing a degree in Fine Arts through a scholarship at the University of Houston. She eventually joined him at his publishing company and that grew into their first business together. After running their company Monday-Thursday, Jessica would tour Thursday-Sunday with Matt's band, running AV and sound engineering. When they decided to start a family, she ran the show while caring for their newborn daughter, Isabella. The successful band toured across the country until Jessica asked, "Is this the limit of our potential?" which resulted in a shift of focus from making great music to building great companies.

Having sold off their publishing company, Jessica founded a full-service ad agency, and soon after, she & Matt co-founded "Mateo's"—the nation's first Mexican food delivery franchise system. Jessica also founded "Kidville," a children's play center and school for the performing hearts and co-founded "Isabella's Sweet Treats" (a wholesale ice cream and dessert company).

With the arrival of their son, Jaxson, came the start of the next chapter of her life. Bella's private school closing ushered in the start of her journey into homeschooling and alternative education. One of the companies to come in this chapter is BrandLync, a fully-integrated digital marketing agency focused on serving a wide variety of clients. In addition to being BrandLync's CEO, Jessica is also CO-CEO of Mead Holdings Group, an angel investor, and partner to more than 20 other companies that she and her husband have acquired and created.

Never straying from her mission to raise full-bellied and hopeful global citizens, Jessica continues to homeschool both children despite their seven-year age difference and her family's constant traveling. A pioneering expert in alternative, supplemental, and customized education, she empowers women globally to be better parents, educators, and CEOs in their personal and business lives through fearless communication.

She is as savvy in business as she is smart in the classroom. Jessica loves to inspire mothers trying to strike the right balance between kids and career, and men who desire to become impactful fathers and leaders. She is also serious about her mission to eradicate child hunger using conscious capitalism, and with her husband, created "Mission E.A.T." to help people all over the world learn how to take control of their ability to earn money and customize their children's education so they can live a life of freedom and choice by design.

Jessica is an intuitive, creative, and nurturing mother, wife, and businesswoman who loves to travel, read, visit national parks, tide pools, zoos, study languages, be by all bodies of water, and most of all dance. In fact, dancing makes her burst with happiness! She, Matt, Bella, and Jaxson are based in Seattle and enjoy spending time at their home in Southern California. You can find more information about Jessica, her platforms, and booking her for speaking engagements at JessicaMead.com.

ENDNOTES

CHAPTER 2

1   Dweck, Carol S. (2006) Mindset: The New Psychology of Success. New York: Random House, c2006.

CHAPTER 3

2   https://foodoppi.com/why-a-growth-mindset-is-crucial-for-success/

CHAPTER 4

3   https://hbr.org/2016/10/how-microsoft-uses-a-growth-mindset-to-develop-leaders

CHAPTER 5

4   https://www.emotivebrand.com/growth-mindset-drives-business/

5   Lareau, Annetta. (2003. Unequal Childhoods: Class, Race, and Family Life. Berkeley: University of California Press.

CHAPTER 7

6   grattan.edu.au/wp-content/uploads/2017/02/Engaging-students-creating-classrooms-that-improve-learning.pdf

CHAPTER 8

7   www.pnas.org/content/114/30/7892

8   www.ted.com/talks/tom_wujec_build_a_tower_build_a_team/transcript

CHAPTER 10

9   www.criticalthinking.org/pages/an-interview-with-linda elder

10   https://eric.ed.gov/?q=California+Teacher+Preparation+for+Instruction+in+Critical+Thinking%3a+Research+Findings+and+Policy+Recommendations&ft=on&id=ED437379

11   Michael Howe. (1997) IQ in Question: The Truth About Intelligence. London: Sage Publications.

12   https://www.davidsongifted.org/search-database/entry/a10857

13   https://www.davidsongifted.org/search-database/entry/a10857

14   www.simplypsychology.org/confirmation-bias.html (confirmation bias)

CHAPTER 12

15   learning.blogs.nytimes.com/2016/02/04/student-question-have-your-parents-and-teachers-given-you-room-to-create/

CHAPTER 16

16   https://greathomeschoolconventions.com/blog/olympic-medalist-simone-biles

17   https://areyoukiddingsocks.com/

18   https://zollipops.com/

19   https://www.youtube.com/user/EvanTubeHD)

20   https://www.hannahgracebeyoutiful.com/

21   http://www.laniboobath.com/

22   https://www.bizjournals.com/boston/inno/stories/inno-insights/2020/09/24/25-under-25-young-entrepreneurs-boston-2020.html

CHAPTER 17

23   https://thesecondprinciple.com/instructional-design/types-of-curriculum/

24   https://theeducationcafe.wordpress.com/2009/11/12/five-basic-types-of-curriculum/

A free ebook edition is available with the purchase of this book.

To claim your free ebook edition:

1. Visit MorganJamesBOGO.com
2. Sign your name CLEARLY in the space
3. Complete the form and submit a photo of the entire copyright page
4. You or your friend can download the ebook to your preferred device

A **FREE** ebook edition is available for you or a friend with the purchase of this print book.

CLEARLY SIGN YOUR NAME ABOVE

Instructions to claim your free ebook edition:
1. Visit MorganJamesBOGO.com
2. Sign your name CLEARLY in the space above
3. Complete the form and submit a photo of this entire page
4. You or your friend can download the ebook to your preferred device

Print & Digital Together Forever.

Snap a photo

Free ebook

Read anywhere

9 781631 955518